Theory and Methods
a Guide for the Beginner

Philip Jones

UNWIN HYMAN

Published by
UNWIN HYMAN LIMITED
15/17 Broadwick Street
London W1V 1FP

© Philip Jones 1985
First published by University Tutorial Press Limited 1985
Reprinted by Bell & Hyman 1987
Reprinted by Unwin Hyman Limited 1990

All rights reserved. No part of this publication may be reproduced, stored in a retrieval system, or transmitted in any form or by any means, electronic, mechanical, photocopying, recording or otherwise, without the prior permission of Unwin Hyman Limited.

ISBN 0 7135 2785 4

Printed and bound in Great Britain by
Billing & Sons Ltd., Worcester

Contents

	Page
Chapter 1 Introduction to Sociological Theories	1
Chapter 2 Functionalism	22
Chapter 3 Marxist Theory	43
Chapter 4 Interpretivism	60
Chapter 5 Theory and Method in Sociology	80
Examination Questions	116
Bibliography	118
Index	120

Preface

Issues of theory and method occupy a central place in contemporary sociology. Any decent understanding of the subject today requires a familiarity with the quite large range of alternative, and sometimes competing, ways in which sociologists theorise about, and research into, their subject matter. This is clearly reflected in the constitution of modern A level syllabuses. For example, not only are a quarter of the questions in the AEB examinations directly concerned with theory and method but a consideration of theory and method throughout the examination is specifically encouraged in the syllabus.

This book is intended simply as a beginners' guide to theory and method in sociology. It attempts only to introduce the beginning student to the basic elements in different sociological perspectives and in no way claims to be more sophisticated than this.

Philip Jones
CCAT Cambridge

Acknowledgements

The author and publisher are grateful to the following for the use of copyright material:

Routledge & Kegan Paul   *Argonauts of the Western Pacific* Bronislaw Malinowski (1922)   pages 29–30; Thomas Nelson & Sons Ltd 'Listening to Conversation' from page 64 of *Perspectives on Society* edited by Roland Meigham et. al.   page 77; George Allen and Unwin *Perspectives in Sociology*   Cuff and Payne (1984)   pages 82, 102–3; 'Talking about Prison Blues'   Cohen and Taylor (1977) in *Doing Sociological Research*   Bell and Newby   Pages 94–5, 103, 106–7; David Rose, Howard Newby, Gordon Marshall and Carolyn Vergler, 'The British Questionnaire' Technical Paper 3, International Project on Class Structure and Class Consciousness: British Project, Dept of Sociology, University of Essex, 1984   pages 89–90; *Asylums* Erving Goffman   Pelican Books 1968   pages 7–8   Copyright © Erving Goffman, 1961, reprinted by permission of Penguin Books Ltd pages 96–97, 113; Extracts published by permission of Transaction, Inc from *Sociological Work* by Howard Becker, copyright © 1976 by Transaction, Inc   page 97; Jonathan Cape Limited   *The Rachel Papers*   Martin Amis   pages 52–3; an extract reprinted by permission of Macmillan Publishing Company from *Meaning and Social Life* Paul Filmer, David Walsh, Michael Phillipson, originally published by Cassell and Co Ltd, © Paul Filmer et al 1972   page 78; The Joint Matriculation Board (5 Advanced Level Questions), The Associated Examining Board (4 Advanced Level Questions), University of Cambridge Local Examinations Syndicate (2 Advanced Level Questions), pages 116–117.

Despite every effort, the publishers have not, as yet, heard from Fontana concerning permission for the extract by Marvin Harris on pages 34–35.

For Deborah

1 An Introduction to Sociological Theories

Humans are social beings. Whether we like it or not, nearly everything we do in our lives takes place in the company of others. Few of our activities are truly solitary, scarce are the times when we are really alone. Thus the study of how we are able to interact with one another, and what happens when we do, would seem to be one of the most fundamental concerns of anyone interested in human life.

Yet strangely enough, it has not been until relatively recently—from about the beginning of the nineteenth century onwards—that a specialised interest into this intrinsically *social* aspect of human existence has been undertaken with any seriousness. Before that time, and even since, other kinds of interests have dominated the analysis of human life. Two of the most resilient of such non-social approaches to human behaviour have been 'naturalistic' explanations and 'individualistic' explanations.

Rather than seeing social behaviour as the product of interaction, these theories have concentrated on presumed qualities inherent in individuals. On the one hand, naturalistic explanations suppose that all human behaviour—social interaction included—is a product of inherited dispositions we possess as human animals. We are, like animals, biologically programmed by Nature. On the other, individualistic explanations baulk at such grand generalisations about the inevitability of behaviour. From this point of view we are all 'individual' and 'different'. Explanations of human behaviour must therefore always rest ultimately on the particular and unique psychological qualities of individuals.

Sociological theories of whatever kind can be usefully understood as standing in direct opposition to these kinds of approaches. By looking a little closer at them now and discovering what is wrong or incomplete about them, it will be easier to understand why sociological theories exist.

Naturalistic Theories

Naturalistic explanations of human activity are common enough. For example, in our society it is often argued that it is only natural for a man and a woman to fall in love, get married and have children. It is equally natural for this nuclear family to live as a unit on their own, with the husband going out to work to earn resources for his dependents, while his wife, at least for the early years of her children's lives, devotes herself to looking after them—to being a mother. As they grow up and acquire more independence, it is still only 'natural' for the children to live at home with their parents responsible for them, at least until their late teens. By then it is only natural for them to want to 'leave the nest', to start to 'make their own way in the world' and, in particular, to look for marriage partners. Thus they, too, can start families of their own.

The corollary of these 'natural' practices is that it is somehow *unnatural not* to want to get married, or to marry for reasons other than love. It is equally unnatural for a couple *not* to want to have children, or for wives *not* to want to be mothers, or for mothers *not* to want to devote the whole of their lives to child-rearing. Though it is not right or natural for children to leave home much younger than eighteen, it is certainly not natural for them not to want to leave home at all in order to start a family of their own.

These 'unnatural' desires and practices are common enough in our society. There are plenty of people who prefer to stay single, or 'marry with an eye on the main chance'. There are plenty of women who do not like the idea of motherhood and there are certainly any number of women who do not want to spend their lives solely being wives and mothers. There are plenty of children who want to leave home long before they are eighteen while there are many who are quite happy to stay as members of their parents' household long after that age.

Why is this? If human behaviour is in fact the product of dispositions inherent in the nature of the human beings then why are such deviations from what is 'natural' so common? We can hardly put down the widespread existence of such 'unnatural' patterns of behaviour to some kind of large scale faulty genetic programming!

In any case, why are there so many variations from these notions of 'normal' family practices in other kinds of societies, also populated by humans? Both history and anthropology provide us with stark contrasts in family life. In his book on family life in Medieval Europe, *Centuries of Childhood,* (1973) Philippe Aries paints a picture of marriage, the family and child-rearing which sharply contradicts our notions of normality. Families were not, as they are for us, private and isolated units, cut off socially, and physically separated, from the world at large. Families were deeply embedded in the community, with people living essentially public, rather than private, lives. They lived in households whose composition was constantly shifting; relatives, friends, children, visitors, passers-by and animals all slept under the same roof. Marriage was primarily a means of forging alliances rather than simply the outcome of 'love', while women certainly did not look upon mothering as their sole destiny. Indeed, child-rearing was a far less demanding and onerous task than it is in our world. Children were not cosseted and coddled to anywhere near the extent we consider 'right'. Many more people—both other relatives and the community at large—were involved in child-rearing, and childhood lasted a far shorter time than it does for us. As Aries puts it "... as soon as he had been weaned, or soon after, the child became the natural companion of the adult."

In contemporary non-industrial societies too, there is a vast range of variations in family practices. Here again, marriage is essentially a means of establishing alliances between groups rather than simply a relationship between individuals. Monogamy—one husband and one wife—is only one form of marriage. Polygyny—marriage between a husband and more than one wife—and polyandry—between a wife and more than one husband—is found in many societies. Domestic life is also far more public and communal than it is for us. Each family unit is just a part of a much wider, co-operating, group of mainly blood relatives associated with a local territory, usually a village. As in Medieval Europe, therefore, child-rearing is not considered the principal responsibility of parents alone, but involves a far greater number of people, relatives and non-relatives.

Clearly, then, to hope to explain human life simply by reference to natural impulses common to all is to ignore one crucial fact that sociology directs attention to—human behaviour varies according to the *social* settings in which people find themselves.

Individualistic Theories

What of individualistic explanations? How useful is the argument that behaviour is the product of the psychological make-up of individuals? The employment of this kind of theory is extremely common. For example, success or failure in *education* is often assumed to be merely a reflection of intelligence: bright children succeed and dim children fail. *Criminals* are often taken to be people with certain kinds of personality: they are usually morally deficient individuals lacking any real sense of right or wrong. *Unemployed* people are equally often condemned as 'work-shy', 'lazy' or 'scroungers'—inadequates who would rather 'get something for nothing' than work for it. *Suicide* is seen as the act of an unstable person—an act undertaken when, as coroners put it, 'the balance of the mind was disturbed'. This kind of explanation is seductive for many people and has proved particularly resilient to sociological critique. But a closer look shows it to be seriously flawed.

If educational achievement is simply a reflection of intelligence then why do children from manual workers' homes do so badly compared with children from middle-class homes? It is clearly nonsensical to suggest that doing one kind of job rather than another is likely to determine the *intelligence* of your child. Achievement in education must in some way be influenced by the characteristics of a child's background.

Equally, the fact that the bulk of people convicted of a crime come from certain social categories must cast serious doubt on the 'deficient personality' theory. The conviction rate is highest for young males, especially black, who come from manual working or unemployed backgrounds. Can we seriously believe that criminal *personalities* are likely to be concentrated in such *social* categories? As in the case of educational achievement, it is clear that the commission of crime must somehow be influenced by social factors.

Again, is it likely that the three million or so people presently unemployed are typically uninterested in working when the vast majority of them have been forced out of their jobs by the recession—a collection of social forces quite outside their control?

Suicide would seem to have the strongest case for being explained as a purely psychological act. But if it is simply a question of 'an unsound mind' then why does the rate of suicide vary between societies? Why does it vary between different groups within the same society? Also, why do the rates in groups and societies remain remarkably constant over time? As in our other examples social factors must be exerting some kind of influence; explanations at the level of the personality are clearly not enough.

Variations such as these demonstrate the inadequacy of theories of human behaviour which exclusively emphasise innate natural drives or the unique psychological make-ups of individuals. If nature is at the root of behaviour why does it vary according to social settings? If we are all different individuals acting according to the dictates of unique psychological influences why do different people in the same social circumstances behave similarly and in ways others can understand? Clearly there is a *social* dimension to human existence which requires *sociological* theorising to explain it.

All sociological theories thus have in common an emphasis on the way human belief and action is the product of social influences. Where they differ concerns what these influences are and how they should be investigated and explained. This book is about these differences.

Society as a structure of rules—the influence of culture on behaviour

Imagine you live in a big city. How many people do you know well enough to be able to discuss with others what kinds of people they are? Twenty? Fifty? A hundred? Now consider how many other people you encounter each day whom you know *nothing* about. For example, how many complete strangers do people living in London or Manchester or Birmingham come into contact with each day? On the street, in shops, on buses and trains, in cinemas or discos—everyday life in a big city is a constant encounter with complete strangers. Yet even if city dwellers bothered to reflect on this fact, they do not normally close their front doors behind them quaking with dread about how all these hundreds of strangers are going to behave towards them. Indeed, they will hardly, if ever, think about it. Why? Why do we take our ability to cope with strangers so much for granted? Of course, it is because nearly all the people we encounter in our lives *do* behave in ways we expect. We *expect* bus passengers, shoppers, taxi drivers, passers-by etc. to behave in quite definite ways even though we know nothing about them *personally*. City dwellers in particular—though it is true of all of us to some extent—routinely enter settings where other human beings are going about their business both expecting *not* to know them and yet also *expecting to know how they will behave*. And, more than this, we are nearly always absolutely right in both respects. We are only surprised if we encounter someone who is *not* a stranger—"Fancy meeting you here! Isn't it a small world!"—or if one of these strangers actually does behave strangely—"Mummy, why is that man shouting?"

Why is this? Why do other humans do what we expect of them? Why is *dis*order or the *un*expected among strangers so rare?

Structural-Consensus Theory

The most traditional, and still influential, way in which sociologists have explained the order and predictability in social life has been to see human behaviour as *learnt* behaviour. This approach is known—for reasons that will become apparent—as *Structural-Consensus theory*. The key process this theory emphasises is called *Socialisation*. This term refers to the way in which human beings learn the kinds of social behaviour expected of them in the social settings in which they find themselves. From this point of view, societies differ because the kinds of behaviour considered appropriate in them differ. People in different societies think and behave differently because they have learnt different *rules* about how to behave and think. The same goes for different groups within the same society. The actions and ideas of one group differ from those of another because its members have been socialised into different rules.

Sociologists call the rules which govern thought and behaviour in a society its *Culture*. Culture exists prior to the people who learn it. At birth, humans are confronted by a social world already in existence. Joining this world involves learning 'how things are done' in it. Only by learning the cultural rules of a society can a human interact with other humans. Because they have been similarly socialised, different individuals will behave similarly.

Consensus theory thus argues that a society's cultural rules determine, or *structure,* the behaviour of its members, channelling their actions in certain ways rather than others. They do so in much the same way as the physical construction of a building structures the actions of people inside it. Take the behaviour of students in a school. Once inside the school they will display quite regular patterns of behaviour. They will all walk along its corridors, up and down its stairs, in and out of its classrooms through their doors, and so on. They will, by and large, not attempt to dig through its floors, smash through its walls, or climb out of its windows. Their physical movements are thus *constrained* by the school building. Since this affects all the students similarly, their behaviour inside it is similar—it will exhibit quite definite patterns. For consensus theory, the same is true of social life. Completely different individuals behave similarly in the same social settings because they are equally constrained by the structure of its cultural rules. Though these *social structures* are not visible in the way physical structures are, their impact on those who are socialised into the rules which make them up is just as determining.

The levels at which these cultural rules operate can vary. Some rules, like laws for instance, operate at the level of the whole society and structure the behaviour of everyone who lives in it. Others are much less general than this, structuring the behaviour of people in quite specific social settings. For example, children in a classroom are expected to behave in an orderly and attentive fashion. In the playground much more licence is given them, while away from school their behaviour often bears no resemblance to that expected of them during school hours.

Similarly, when police officers or nurses or members of the armed forces are 'on duty', certain cultural rules structure their behaviour very rigidly. Out of uniform and off duty these constraints do not apply, though other ones do instead—those governing their behaviour as fathers and mothers, husbands and wives, for instance.

This shows how this theory of a social structure of cultural rules operates. The rules apply not to the individuals themselves but to the *positions* in the social structure they occupy. Shoppers, police officers, traffic-wardens, schoolteachers or pupils are constrained by the cultural expectations attached to these positions only when they occupy them. In other circumstances, in other locations in the social structure—as fathers or mothers, squash players, football supporters, Church members— other rules come into play.

The positions in a social structure sociologists call its *roles*. The rules which structure the behaviour of their occupants are called *norms*. Some cultural rules are not attached to any particular role or set of roles. Called *values,* these are in a sense summaries of approved ways of living which act as a kind of base from which particular norms spring. So, for example, 'Education is the Key to Success'; 'Family Relationships are the most Important to Protect'; 'Self-help is the Means to Individual Fulfilment'; all these are values which provide general principles from which norms directing behaviour in schools and colleges, in the home and at work are derived.

According to this sociological theory, socialisation into norms and values produces an agreement, or *consensus,* between people about appropriate behaviour and belief without which no human society can survive. This is why it is called *Structural-consensus* theory. Through socialisation, cultural rules structure behaviour, guarantee a consensus about expected behaviour, and thereby ensure social order.

Clearly, in a complex society, there are sometimes going to be competing norms and values. For example, while some people think it is wrong for mothers to go out to work, many women see motherhood at best as a real imposition and at worst as an infringement of their liberty. Children often encourage each other to misbehave at school and disapprove of their peers who refuse to. Teachers usually see this very much the other way round! The Tory Party Conference is annually strident in its condemnation of any speaker who criticises the police. Some young blacks in our cities would be equally furious with any of their number who had *other* than a strongly beligerent attitude towards them.

Consensus theorists explain such differences in behaviour and attitude in terms of the existence of alternative cultural influences characteristic of different social settings. A good example of this emphasis is their approach to *educational inequality.*

Educational research demonstrates, in the most conclusive fashion, that achievement in education is strongly linked to class membership, gender and race. To take class as our example, there is over-whelming evidence that working-class children of similar intelligence to children from middle-class backgrounds nevertheless achieve far less academically than their middle-class counterparts.

To explain this, consensus theorists naturally turn to the stock concepts in their approach to social life-norms, values, socialisation and culture. Starting from the basic assumption that behaviour and belief is caused by socialisation into particular rules, their explanation of working-class under-achievement in education seeks to identify
(i) the cultural influences which propel middle-class children to academic success;
(ii) the cultural influences which drag working-class children down to mediocrity.

Briefly, the argument usually goes something like this. The upbringing of middle-class children involves socialisation into norms and values which are ideal for educational achievement. Because of their own likely educational experiences, middle-class parents will be very knowledgeable about how education works and how to make the most of it. Further, they are likely to be very keen for their children to make a success of their own education. These children will thus grow up in a social setting where educational achievement is valued and where they will be constantly encouraged and assisted to fulfil their academic potential.

In contrast, the home background of working-class children often lacks such advantageous socialisation. Working-class parents are likely to have had only limited, and possibly unhappy, experiences of education. Even if they are keen for their children's educational success they will almost certainly lack the know-how of the middle-class parent to make this happen. Indeed, sometimes they may actively disapprove of academic attainment: for instance, they may simply distrust what they do not know. As a result, their children may well be taught instead to value the more immediate and practical advantages of leaving school as soon as possible. For example, boys may be encouraged to 'learn a trade'—to eschew academic success for the security of an apprenticeship in 'a proper job'. Here is a clear example of the application of consensus theory to the facts of social life. Different patterns of behaviour are the product of different patterns of socialisation. Now it might seem that this contradicts the commitment of such theorists to the idea of social order in a society as the outcome of an agreement or a consensus among its members about how to behave and what to think. But consensus theorists say that despite differences of culture between different groups, even despite *opposing sub-cultures* within the overall culture, in all societies an *overall* consensus prevails. This is because all societies have certain values about whose importance there is *no* dispute. Called either *Central Values* or *Core Values,* socialisation ensures everyone conforms to them. In Victorian Britain, perhaps two such central values were a commitment to Christian Morality and Loyalty to the Queen and Empire. Today examples of central values might be the Importance of Economic Growth, the Importance of Democratic Institutions, the Importance of the Rule of Law, and the Importance of the Freedom of the Individual within the Law. (Indeed, anything trotted out as 'basic to the British Way of Life' at any particular time is usually a good bet for a central value in Britain).

For consensus theory then, central values are the backbone of social structures built and sustained by the process of socialisation. Social behaviour and social order are determined by the fact of external cultural forces. Human social life is possible because of the existence of social structures of cultural rules.

Society as a structure of inequality — the influence of advantages on behaviour

Other sociologists argue a rather different theoretical case. They agree that society determines our behaviour by structuring or constraining it. Byt they emphasise different structural constraints. For them, the most important influence on social life is the impact on behaviour of the distribution of advantage. Where advantages are unequally distributed, the capacities of the advantaged to choose how to behave are much greater than those of the disadvantaged.

For example, while it is perfectly feasible for two boys of the same intelligence to be equally keen to fulfil their potential in education, and to be equally encouraged by their parents, the fact of this culturally instilled enthusiasm cannot by itself tell us everything about their potential educational success or failure. From this theoretical point of view, if one boy comes from a wealthy home while the other from a much poorer one, this is far more significant for their educational chances than their similar (learnt) desire. Clearly, the unequal distribution of advantage—in this case material resources—will assist the privileged boy and hamper the disadvantaged boy.

The advantaged boy can be bought a private education, while the poorer boy cannot. The advantaged boy can be assured of living in a substantial enough house with sufficient space to study whereas the disadvantaged boy may have to make do with the room with a television in it, or a bedroom shared with his brothers and sisters. The advantaged boy can rely on a proper diet and resulting good health whereas children from poor backgrounds often cannot. The advantaged boy can be guaranteed access to all the books and equipment he needs to study whereas the poorer boy cannot. Probably most important, the advantaged boy will be able to continue his education up to the limit of his potential unhindered. For those less advantaged, it is often the need to leave school and go out to work to add to the family income that is the stronger impulse, usually bringing their education to a premature end.

Structural-Conflict Theory

So one primary objection some sociologists have to structural-consensus theory is that where societies are unequal, people are not *only* constrained by the norms and values they have learnt via socialisation. They are also constrained by the *advantages* they possess—by their positions in the *structures of inequality* within their society. This emphasis, on the effects on behaviour of an unequal distribution of advantage in a society, is usually associated with *structural-conflict theory*. Why are such theories *conflict* theories?

The kinds of inequality structures in a society can vary. Races can be unequal, young and old can be unequal, men and women can be unequal, people doing different jobs can be unequal, people of different religious beliefs can be unequal etc. etc. The kinds of advantages unequally possessed by such groups can vary too. Different groups can possess unequal amounts of power, or authority, or prestige, or wealth, or a combination of these, and other, advantages.

Notwithstanding the kinds of inequality conflict theories focus on and the kinds of advantage they see as unequally distributed, such theories have in common the axiom that the origin and persistence of a structure of inequality lies in the domination of its disadvantaged groups by its advantaged ones. Conflict theories have their name because for them, inherent in an unequal society is a *conflict of interests* between its haves and its have-nots. As Wes Sharrock puts it: "The conflict view is ... founded upon the assumption that ... any society ... may provide extraordinarily good lives for some but this is usually only possible because the great majority are oppressed and degraded ... Differences of *interest* are therefore as important to society as agreements upon rules and values, and most societies are so organised that they not only provide greater benefits for some than for others but in such a way that the accrual of benefits to a few causes positive discomfort to others." (In Worsley (ed.)

An Introduction to Sociological Theories

So conflict theory differs from consensus theory not only because it is interested in the way an unequal distribution of advantage in a society structures behaviour. It also differs because it is interested in the conflict, not consensus, inherent in such a society. According to a conflict theory, there is a conflict of interest between a society's advantaged and disadvantaged, which is inherent in their relationship.

There is another conflict theory objection to consensus theory too. Conflict theorists not only accuse consensus theory of being over-interested in norms and values as determinants of behaviour at the expense of other influences. They also argue that consensus theory misunderstands the role of its key concern—socialisation into culture. Consensus theory argues that people behave as they do because they have been socialised into cultural rules. The outcome is a consensus about how to think and behave which manifests itself in patterns and regularities of behaviour. Conflict theorists argue that we should see the role of cultural rules and the process of socialisation in a very different light. The real structural determinants of behaviour are the rewards and advantages possessed unequally by different groups in a society. Such a structure of unequally distributed advantages is plainly and clearly unfair. Other things being equal, those most disadvantaged by it would not put up with such a state of affairs.

Normally, however, other things are *not* equal. Where a society is unequal, the only way it can survive is if those who are disadvantaged in it are forced to accept their deprivation. Sometimes this force involves naked coercion. Plenty of unequal societies survive because their rulers maintain repressive regimes based on terror. The exercise of the force necessary to maintain unequal advantage need not take such an obvious or naked form. Structures of inequality can also survive—and with a surer future—if somehow those most disadvantaged by them can be prevented from seeing themselves as under-privileged. Or, if they do recognise it, if they can be persuaded that this is fair enough—rightful, legitimate and just. The way this happens is through the control and manipulation of the norms and values—the cultural rules—into which people are socialised.

In effect then, for the conflict theorist, socialisation is more likely to be an instrument of force and domination, rather than the means to consensus and social order.

Imagine the following scenario. It is early morning in a Latin American country. A group of agricultural labourers, both men and women, are waiting by a roadside for a bus to arrive to drive them to work. Suddenly two vans draw up and four hooded men jump out. At gunpoint they order the labourers into the backs of the vans which then race away deep into the surrounding countryside. At nightfall they are abandoned and the labourers transferred into a large covered lorry. This is driven through the night deep into the mountains. Before day-break it reaches its destination—a huge underground mine, built deep into the heart of a mountain. Here the labourers are horrified to find a vast army of slaves toiling away, under constant surveillance by brutal guards. After being given a meagre meal, the labourers are forced to join this workforce.

As they live out their desperate lives within this mountain world, some of the slaves try to escape. When caught they are publicly punished as a deterrent to the others. Two attempts to escape result in public execution. As the labourers get older, they rely on each other for companionship and their memories for comfort. They keep sane by recounting stories of their former lives. In the fullness of time, children are born to them. Their parents are careful to tell these children all about their past. As these children grow up and have children of *their* own, they, too, are told these tales of their grandparents' land of lost content. But for them these are handed-down historical stories, not tales based on experience. As the years go by, though the facts of life within the mountain remain the same, the perception of life in it by the participants alters. By the time five or six generations of slaves have been born their knowledge of the world of their ancestors' past lives has become considerably dimmed. It is still talked about, sometimes. But by now it is a misted world of folklore and myth. All they know from experience is slavery. So far as any of them can remember, they have always been slaves. In their world, slavery is *'normal'*. In effect, to be a slave has come to mean something very different for them from what it had meant for their original ancestors.

A similar process occurs with the oppressors. As the view of themselves held by the slaves has become altered over time, the necessity for naked force has become less and less. As, through socialisation, their subordinates have begun to acquiesce in their own subordination, the guards no longer brandish their guns and clubs. Because of *this,* they no longer see *them*selves as the original guards had done. Both dominant and subordinate, knowing nothing else, have, through socialisation, come to see the facts of the inequality in their world in a very different light from its original inhabitants.

Though this story is rather larger than life, its telling does allow us to see the role of socialisation into cultural rules as conflict theorists see it. Their argument is that we must be careful not to dismiss the presence of conflict in societies just because a consensus *seems* to prevail. Naked force is only necessary so long as people see themselves as oppressed. If

An Introduction to Sociological Theories

they can be persuaded that they are not oppressed or if they fail to see that they are, then they can be willing architects in the design of their own subordination. The easiest way to exercise power, and gain advantage as a result, is for the dominated to be unaware of the fact of its existence.

Rather than simply *describe* cultural rules in a society, therefore, we must carefully examine their content. We must ask "who *benefits* from this *particular* set of rules prevailing in this society rather than some other set?" Cultural rules cannot be neutral or somehow all-benevolent. Of course people *are* socialised into pre-existing norms and values. But this tells us only half the story. We must also find out whether some groups *benefit more than others* from the existence of a particular set of rules and have a greater say in their construction and interpretation. If they do, then the process of socialisation into these is an instrument of their advantage.

For example, even a cursory glance at the kinds of occupations dominated by women and the kinds of rewards they receive for doing them clearly indicates the advantages men have over women in our kind of society. A female Prime Minister, the odd female Civil Servant or M.P. or Judge or University Vice-Chancellor cannot hide the facts of unequal occupational opportunity and unequal economic rewards based on gender. The facts are that males dominate the best rewarded and most prestigious occupations and (despite the Equal Opportunities Commission) usually receive greater rewards when they *do* do the same jobs as women.

Clearly, there is considerable potential conflict of interests between men and women here. It is in men's interests for women not to compete in large numbers for the limited number of highly rewarded jobs. It is in their interests for women to stay at home and provide domestic services for them. If women were to want something different, this would be in conflict with the desires and ambitions of men.

So why is it that so many women do *not* object to this state of affairs? If women are as systematically deprived of occupational opportunities and rewards by men as this, why do so many of them acquiesce in their deprivation? For example, why are some of the fiercest critics of the Feminist movement women? Why do so many women *choose* to be (unpaid) houseworkers for the benefit of their husbands and children? Why do so many girls *choose* domestic science, needlework and art at school in preference to, say, chemistry, physics or maths? Why is the extent of so many girls' ambitions to 'start a family'? Why do they not wish to explore their potential in other activities instead or as well?

Clearly, a substantial part of the answers to these questions is that

13

women have been socialised into accepting this definition of themselves. For conflict theorists here is a clear example of particular norms and values working in the interests of one section of society and against another. Through the ideas they have learnt, women have been forced to accept a role which is subordinate to men.

There is one final question to be asked about this theoretical approach. How does the exercise of force by means of socialisation into particular ideas happen? Conflict theorists say it can be intentional or unintentional. The rulers of any number of societies in the world today deliberately employ *propaganda* designed to persuade the ruled of the legitimacy of this arrangement. They also often control and *censor* the mass media of their countries to ensure a lack of opposition to this controlled socialisation.

The exercise of this kind of force can be less deliberate too. Take our example of the inequality between men and women in our society. To what extent does the image of women presented in advertising promote an acceptance of this inequality? Though the intention is to sell various products—from lingerie and perfume to household goods to alcohol and cigarettes to cars and office equipment—the images of women used in this advertising are so particular that it has other, less intentional effects too. Two images dominate. One is of the woman as the domestic at home using the 'best' products to clean, polish, launder and cook. The other is of the woman as sexually desirable, guaranteed to either (i) magically adorn the life of any male who is sensible enough to drink X gin, drive Y car or use Z shaving lotion; or (ii) transform into a similarly irresistible seductress any woman who wears A underwear, drinks B alcohol, wears C perfume or gets given D box of chocolates.

Such advertising socialises both men *and* women of course. The outcome is a stereotypical view of womanhood and of the place of women in society embraced not only by those whom it disadvantages but also by those who benefit from it. There *is* a consensus about such things, therefore. However, it is not the kind of consensus portrayed by the consensus theorist. It is an *imposed* consensus, preventing the conflict that would break out if people were allowed to see the world as it *really* is.

There are a number of sociological theories which could be called structural-conflict, in that they are based on two main premises:
1 Social structures consist of unequally advantaged groups. The interests of these groups are in conflict since inequality results from the domination and exploitation of disadvantaged groups by advantaged ones.
2 Social order in such societies is maintained by force—either by actual

force or by force exercised through socialisation.

Easily the most famous and influential of such theories argues that the most important advantages that are possessed unequally in societies are *economic* or *material* advantages. Socialisation into cultural rules is the major means by which such structures of economic inequality and the relationships of domination that characterise them are sustained. This theory is Marxist theory, the subject of Chapter 3.

In structural-consensus theory and structural-conflict theory, then, we have emphases on different kinds of influence on people's thought and behaviour. Though both theories see the origin of human social life in the influences or determinants of an outside society, they disagree about what this outside society consists of. Consensus theory argues for the primacy of the influence of culture—what we come to learn to want to do as a result of socialisation. Conflict theory argues, in contrast, for most attention to be paid to the conflict inherent in the relationship between unequally-advantaged groups in society, and for the content of culture to be seen as a means of perpetuating these relationships of inequality.

Society as the creation of its members— the influence of interpretation on behaviour

Our third kind of sociological theory leads us in a rather different direction. It still attempts to explain why human beings in society behave in the ways they do. But instead of looking for the answer in the influence of an outside society which people confront and are constrained by, this theory argues something else. From this point of view, the most important influence on an individual's behaviour is the behaviour of *other* individuals towards him or her. The focus is not on general cultural rules or on the unequal distribution of advantage in whole societies. It is on the way individual pieces of social interaction proceed; on how the parties to them are able to understand one another. This is not to say that structural theories do not try to explain this too. For consensus theory, for example, we behave towards each other as role players and we act out the parts we have learnt through socialisation. But how do we decide *which* roles to play in *which* social setting? Consensus theory does not try to explain why people choose one role rather than another. It is assumed that we are somehow programmed to make the right choices. Our third kind of theory, however, argues that the choice of role playing is a much more complex process than this rather robotised view. Indeed, it argues, the *essence* of social life lies in the quite extraordinary abilities only humans possess to *work out what is going on around them,* and then *to choose to act in a particular way in the light of this interpretation.* Such theories are called *interpretive.*

Interpretive theory

Interpretivists stress the need to concentrate on the *micro*-level of social life—the way particular individuals are able to interact with one another—rather than on the *macro*-level—the way the whole structure of society influences the behaviour of individuals. They argue that we must not think societies exist outside of and prior to the interaction of individuals. For interpretivists, societies are the *end result* of human interaction, not its cause. Only by looking at how individual humans are able to interact can we come to understand how social order is created. To see how this happens, let us reflect on the kinds of action of which humans are capable.

Some human action is like the action of phenomena in the inanimate world—purpose*less,* or lacking intention. We all do things *in*voluntarily—without making a decision to—like sneezing, blinking, yawning. We do not *choose* to feel fear, or excitement, or pain, or choose to react in certain ways to those feelings. In effect we behave as tulips do when they respond to light and open their leaves, or water does when it reaches a certain temperature and freezes.

So far as we know, the actions of non-human *animate* phenomena are purely instinctive—automatic or reflex responses to external stimulii—too. It is true that animals, for example, often *appear* to act in a purposive way by using their brains. They seem to *choose* to eat or sleep or be friendly or aggressive or evacuate their bladders over the new living-room carpet. However, the usual zoological explanation is that even these often quite sophisticated patterns of animal action are *in*voluntary. They are *re*active and programmed rather than the product of voluntary creative decision-making.

Nearly all human action *is* voluntary. It is the product of a conscious decision to act, a result of thought. Nearly everything we do is the result of choosing to act in one way rather than another. Furthermore, this is purposive, or goal-oriented choice. We choose between courses of action because, as humans, we are able to aim at an end or a goal and take action to achieve this. Nearly all human action, that is, is *meaningful* action: we *mean* to do what we do in order to achieve our chosen purposes.

Where do these chosen purposes, our goals, come from? What

An Introduction to Sociological Theories

interpretivism emphasises is that we decide what to do *in the light of our interpretation of the world around us.* Being human means walking around the world making sense of the settings or situations in which we find ourselves and choosing to act accordingly. To use the usual interpretivist phrase for this, we choose what to do in the light of our 'definition of the situation'. For example, say you wake on a summer's morning to find the sun shining in a cloudless sky. You decide to sunbathe all day and to mow your lawn in the evening, when it will be cooler. At lunchtime, you see large clouds beginning to form in the distance. Because you decide there is a chance of a thunderstorm you cut the grass immediately. You get very hot. It does not rain. In the evening, you go for a walk in the country. You come to a country pub and stop for a drink. As you sit outside you notice smoke rising on a hillside some distance away. As you watch the smoke gets thicker and darker. You decide the fire is unattended and out of control. You dash inside the pub and ring the Fire Brigade. Shortly afterwards you hear a fire engine racing to the fire. You climb a nearby hill to have a better look. When you get there you see that the fire is in fact being deliberately burnt in the garden of a house on the hillside you had been unable to see from the pub. Shortly afterwards you hear the fire engine returning to its base. You go back to the pub to finish your drink. It has been cleared away in your absence. You have no more money. You decide it is not your day. You decide to go home.

Of course, most of the settings we have to make sense of in life involve more than this. As was remarked in the first paragraph of this chapter, nearly everything we do in our lives takes place in the company of others. Most of the situations we have to define in order to choose how to act involve *other* humans doing things. We see a very large man shaking his fist and shouting at us and decide that he is not overjoyed that we have driven into the back of his car. As a result we decide not to suggest that he was responsible for the accident because of the way he had parked. We see a traffic warden slipping a parking ticket under our windscreen wiper and decide not to contribute to the Police Benevolent Fund after all. This is *social* action. It is action we choose to take in the light of what we interpret the behaviour of others to mean.

There is more to social action than just interpretation leading to action, however. Most of the time when we interact with other humans they *want* us to arrive at certain interpretations of their actions—they *want* us to think one thing of them rather than another. The man whose car we have just bashed is not behaving in the rather distinctive manner described above because he wishes us to come round to his house for tea. The man scratching his nose in the auction room is not alleviating an

17

itch. He is communicating his bid to the auctioneer, and he expects the latter will interpret his actions as he wishes. Pedestrians in London streets do not wave to taxi-drivers because they are, or want to become, their friends. They do so to ensure the taxi-drivers know they want a lift.

Dress can often organise interpretation just as effectively as gestures too of course. Though the punk rocker, the skinhead, the bowler-hatted civil servant, the policeman and the traffic warden whom we encounter in the street make no *apparent* attempt to communicate with us, they are certainly doing so nevertheless. They may want us to think certain things about them when we see them, so they choose to communicate by the use of uniforms. They are making a symbolic use of dress, if you like; after all, garments symbolise, as do people's gestures, what their users want us to interpret about them.

The most effective symbols of meaning humans have at their disposal are words—*linguistic* symbols. Though dress, gesture, touch and even smell can often communicate our meanings and organise the interpretations of others adequately enough, clearly the most efficient—and most remarkable—way in which we can get others to understand us is through language. This is why interpretivists are so often interested in the ways humans use language to exchange meanings with each other. Language, verbal or written, is the uniquely human device which we are able to use in order to interact meaningfully with one another and thereby create what we call society.

From this point of view, societies are made up of individuals engaging in a countless number of meaningful encounters. The result is social order. But this is no *determined* order. It is not the result of the imposition of cultural rules as the consensus theorist sees it. Nor is it the result of the constraints of a world where advantages are unequally distributed, and where cultural rules legitimate these constraints, as the conflict theorist sees it. Instead, it is an order created, or accomplished, by the capacities of a society's members themselves. It is the end result of occasions of interaction carried on by interpreting, meaning-attributing actors who can make sense of the social settings in which they find themselves and who choose courses of action accordingly.

There is another important difference between the structural and interpretive conceptions of society. For the structuralist, the character of a society—its social structure—is not in doubt. It is a 'real' thing which exists outside of its members. For the interpretivist however, it is much more difficult to describe a society which is the outcome of interpretation as somehow 'true' or 'real' in the way structural theorists conceive of their social structures.

As we have been stressing, being a human for the interpretivist involves interpreting what is going on around one—saying "This is what is happening here"—and choosing an appropriate course of action in the light of this interpretation. Such interpretations of 'what is going on here' can only ever be considered 'correct' or 'true' for the particular person doing the interpreting. What is 'really' going on depends on the way it is seen and interpreted by a particular individual.

Reality is indeed in the eye of the beholder. We act in ways *we* consider appropriate. What we consider appropriate depends upon what *we* think the behaviour of others *means*. It is therefore by no means inconceivable that other people, in exactly the same social situations as ourselves, would have taken the behaviour going on around them to mean something very different and therefore to have taken very different courses of action from those we chose. For example, say a car crashes into a wall on a wet winter's evening. The police officer called to the scene discovers a dead driver and a strong smell of drink in the car. A search reveals an empty whisky bottle underneath a seat. As any human being inevitably does upon encountering any social situation, the officer engages in a process of interpretation, defining this situation. Weighing up the evidence, he or she decides that the crash was an accident caused by a combination of the driver being drunk and losing control of the vehicle in difficult driving conditions. *Another* officer called to the scene might have interpreted things rather differently however. He or she might have considered the possibility that the driver deliberately drove the car into the wall as an act of suicide, having first given himself the dutch courage to do so by drinking the whisky. Because things are seen (at least potentially) differently from the first police officer, the second officer makes enquiries the first would not have bothered to. The dead man's domestic and work affairs are looked into and it is discovered that he had recently separated from his wife, losing custody of his children. The officer decides that suspicions of suicide are sufficiently confirmed by this additional evidence to say so in the Coroner's Court.

How the death is finally interpreted depends upon the decision of the Court of course, when the evidence is reassessed by a new set of interpreters—particularly the Coroner. The Coroner's decision will define the death as either accidental or a suicide. Is the judgment the 'truth'? Who is to say what was the 'reality' of the situation defined by the human beings who came across it? In the case of this kind of example of course, no-one can ever know.

Even in less inconclusive circumstances, action still always depends upon the interpretation of the particular beholder. Say you come across a middle-aged man grappling with a young girl in the bushes of a park. What you do depends on what you think is going on, of course. You may decide the man is assaulting the girl and take a course of action you see fit in the light of this interpretation (and depending how brave you feel at the time!). Or, you may decide it's just a bit of fun between friends, or horseplay between lovers, or a father admonishing his daughter—or any other interpretation that may spring to your mind. What matters is not so much that you are *right,* that you see what is *really* happening, but that

1   you cannot help but come to some sort of interpretation or other (even if it is that you do *not* know what is happening) and
2   what you decide to do will be the result of this interpretation.

Though subsequent events may 'prove' things one way or another, initial action undertaken by human beings in such social cirumstances, though always involving such a process of interpretation, can never be assumed to be definitely 'true' or 'real'. It can only ever be how we *choose* to see things. The world 'is' what we think it is. As W.I. Thomas puts it, "If man defines situations as real, they are real in their consequences". In contrast to the structuralist view, the social 'reality' is not a factual, objective, unambiguous state of affairs. It can only ever be what the actors involved in interaction *think* is real, since what they *think* is real determines what they decide to do. Reality is therefore quite definitely the creation of individuals. Furthermore, because social worlds so created are dependent on the arbitrary interpretations of particular individuals in particular social settings, they are much more precarious and fortuitous constructions than the notion of social structures determining behaviour suggests.

Conclusions

Let us summarise our discussion so far and look ahead to the rest of the book. Differences between sociological theories can be usefully understood as centring on the adequacy of the *deterministic* approach to social life of structural theory. The questions to be asked of this kind of approach are of two kinds. The first is this. If societies do exist as structures which individuals encounter upon being born and which determine their behaviour, then how can we best theorise about these social structures? What *kind* of determinants of behaviour do societies consist of?

As we have seen, there are two fundamentally opposed kinds of structural theory—structural-consensus theory and structural-conflict theory. The best known kind of consensus theory is *Functionalism.* The best known kind of conflict theory is *Marxist theory.* We shall look at

Functionalism in Chapter 2 and at Marxist theory in Chapter 3.

The second question about structural theory is not about the nature of social structures but about whether they exist at all. It is this. Is it *true* that societies exist as structures outside their members, determining their behaviour? Or do human beings actively create and reproduce what we call society because they alone among living things possess the ability to interpret and communicate meaning?

So far as this question is concerned we have already seen that the anti-determinist flag in sociology is flown by interpretive theories. The best known of these are *Symbolic-Interactionism, Labelling Theory* and *Ethnomethodology*. We shall be looking at them in Chapter 4.

In chapter 5 we shall extend our discussion to consider the problems faced by sociologists in trying to produce knowledge about social life—i.e. the problems concerned with how they go about producing data by research. Obviously how you produce knowledge about social behaviour depends upon what you think social behaviour *is*. Inevitably, therefore, debates about how to do research cannot be separated from the theoretical debates discussed in the other chapters in the book.

Though it is rather over-simplifying things, it will do for now to say that in general structural theorists—who believe in the existence of an external, determining society—will be more likely to support the use of the methods and procedures of *science* (as used in the natural and physical sciences) to produce data about human behaviour. Those who *deny* the existence of such structures—interpretivists—will be more likely to argue that the methods and procedures of science are wholly *in*appropriate for the study of human social life. Sociologists who support the application of science to the study of society are called *positivists,* because *positivism* is the name usually given to the set of assumptions underpinning the activity we call science.

So, to recast the earlier paragraph, we can say that *structural theorists are more likely to be positivist whereas interpretive theorists are more likely to be anti-positivist.*

This is how the remainder of the book is organised. Now, on to Chapter 2 and functionalism.

2 Functionalism

Functionalism is the best known structural-consensus theory. It is inextricably bound up with the work of its first major exponent, Frenchman Emile Durkheim. Other significant functionalists have been the leading British social anthropologists in the years between 1920 and 1960. Of particular importance has been the work of anthropology's first two major figures, Bronislaw Malinowski and A.R. Radcliffe-Brown. In addition the later writings of anthropologists like E.E. Evans-Pritchard, Meyer Fortes and Max Gluckman all helped to firmly establish functionalist theory in British social science.

In twentieth century sociology, undoubtedly the major figure (from the 1930's to the late 1950's) has been the American functionalist Talcott Parsons, though other U.S. functionalists like R.K. Merton amd Kingsley Davis have been important too. Until the 1960's America dominated sociology, and social anthropology dominated British social science. So, from the years between the early 1920's and the late 1950's, though our other theoretical perspectives had long been in existence, they had little impact. The theoretical stage was dominated by the functionalist version of structural-consensus theory.

Though it has since been knocked off its pedestal by the opposition, particularly outside the U.S., an understanding of contemporary theoretical alternatives in sociology must begin with an understanding of functionalism. In a very real sense, the rise to prominence of conflict theory, mainly in the form of Marxist theory, and the emergence of interpretive theories like symbolic-interactionism and ethnomethodology as major sociological approaches can only be understood in the light of the criticisms that began to be made (and by the late 1950's, very loudly) of functionalism. Conflict theory and interpretivism did not come into being in opposition to functionalism. However, they rose to prominence (at least in the West, in the case of conflict theory) when they did because for many sociologists they provided questions and answers about social life which they had come to realise functionalism could not. Let us see why.

Emile Durkheim: the origins and characteristics of functionalism

As we have seen, the analysis of social forces at work outside of, and independent of, the biological and psychological characteristics of people is a taken-for-granted interest for structural sociology today. Such a theory had no real currency in human thought until the end of the eighteenth century and the rise of sociology, and was never well-established until the work of Emile Durkheim.

Durkheim had a quite orthodox consensus view of social structures. Their crucial feature, he said, is that they are made up of *norms* and *values*—cultural definitions of behaviour considered appropriate and worthy in different settings. Since it is through socialisation that we learn these normative definitions, it is only this process which makes individuals members of society and, therefore, makes social life possible.

According to Durkheim, though we may *think* we choose to behave in one way rather than another, in reality the choice is made for us. It was Durkheim who first of all stressed the consensus view that (as Lucy Mair puts it) "Even the possibilities of thought and experience are *inherited*, not invented". For example, people who attend a religious service may believe in their God as sincerely and as subjectively as humans can. But the beliefs and practices of their religion were in existence before they were—they *learnt* them. Like all other social acitivity, religious beliefs and practices are structured by society and by peoples' positions in it . This is how Durkheim himself makes this point, so fundamental to the consensus view of social life. "When I fulfil my obligations as brother, husband, or citizen I perform duties which are defined, externally to myself and my acts, in law and custom. Even if they conform to my own sentiments, and I feel their reality subjectively, such reality is still objective, for I did not create them; I merely inherited them through my education ... the church member finds the beliefs and practices of his religious life ready made at birth; their existence prior to him implies their existence outside himself".

For Durkheim, then, the achievement of social life among humans, and the existence of social order in society—which he calls "social solidarity"—is ensured by culture—collective standards or rules of behaviour. (Durkheim's phrase for these rules was "social facts"). Although these are only *visible* through the conformity of individuals to them, they are, nevertheless, in Durkheim's words, "external to, and constraining upon" these individuals. Though not capable of being seen, such structures of cultural rules are as real to the individuals whose behaviour is determined by them as the world's physical structure which they also confront. Society, in a famous phrase of Durkheim's, is a reality *"sui generis"*—it has its own existence.

Such a deterministic view of individual behaviour raises a real problem, however. If society is a structure of cultural rules which *pre-exists* individuals and determines their behaviour, where do these rules come from? How do social structures come into being and why do they have the cultural characteristics they do? The content of a society's culture cannot be explained as the product of people's choices since the consensus view is that these choices are themselves part of the culture. It is only through socialisation that people learn them, as they learn all other cultural prescriptions for belief and action. Clearly, in order to explain the existence of cultural rules, the consensus theorist has to find some answer other than the purposive intentions of individuals. For Durkheim, and for most consensus theorists since, the answer lies in a theory called Functionalism.

The organismic analogy

According to Durkheim, we can best understand the existence and character of social structures by comparing them to the origins and workings of biological organisms. As the name suggests, an organism is a living entity whose existence and health depends upon all the organs that go to make it up working properly and working together. In the human body, for instance, all the organs are *interdependent*. The workings of the brain depend upon the workings of the lungs, which depend upon the workings of the heart and so on. Furthermore, all (or nearly all, in the case of the human body) these organs are *indispensable*. Each exists because it satisfies a particular need of the human body which no other organ can. For example, the heart exists because of the need for an organ to pump blood round the body, the liver exists because of the need for the blood to be purified, the kidneys exist because of the need to dispose of waste matter and so on. In other words, the reason why each of the constituent parts of the body exists is because each peforms a particular *function* for the overall system. Furthermore, all these necessary parts have to function together in an *integrated* way for the system as a whole to work properly. The difference between referring to integrated wholes as 'systems' rather than 'structures' can be understood as simply the difference between a static picture of the whole—its structure—and what this looks like when it is actually working—as a system. In sociology the terms are often used interchangeably for just this reason. A society both has a structure and works as a system.

Durkheim argues that a social system works like an organic system. Societies are made up of structures of cultural rules—established beliefs and practices—to which their members are expected to conform.

Functionalism

Sociologists describe any established way of thinking or acting in a society into which its members are socialised as being *institutionalised* in that society. For functionalists, the institutions of a society—for example the kind of family form it has, its political arrangements, its educational arrangements, its religious arrangements etc.—are analogous to the parts, the organs, of an organism. Societies consist of parts which are integrated and inter-dependent. As with organs, the reason why an institutionalised way of thinking or acting exists in a society is that it plays an indispensable part—or, to use the functionalist phrase—*performs a necessary function*—in maintaining the society in a satisfactory state. In the case of the human body, if any organ fails to perform properly, ill-health, or even loss of life, is the result. For Durkheim, such a functional failure by an institution—if it malfunctions—also leads to a comparable state for the whole social system. Functionalists have various phrases to describe this—a 'loss of social solidarity', a 'lack of integration', or a 'loss of equilibrium' are three favourite ones.

Crucially, therefore, this account of the origins and workings of societies means that the existence of a social institution, of a part of the social structure, is not the result of *the members of a society deciding* to act or think this way. After all, people do not *decide* to have bowels or a liver or a pair of kidneys. They exist because the body needs them to perform necessary functions. In the same way, in functionalist theory, the institutional arrangements of a society exist not because of any choice on the part of its members. They are there because they are performing a necessary function for the social structure as a whole. Durkheim and other functionalists therefore argue that we should always explain the existence of social arrangements by looking for the *function* being performed by them—for the needs of the social system as a whole they are satisfying.

Durkheim's functional theory of religion

The following is a simple example of the use of functionalist theory taken from one of Durkheim's own works, called *The Elementary Forms of Religious Life.*

There is an aborigine people called the Arunta, who live in Australia. They are divided up into two kinds of group. *Bands* are their domestic groups who live together day to day, eking out a meagre survival by hunting and gathering in the bush. The Arunta also belong to much larger groups, called *Clans*. Much like the Scottish clans of great importance long ago, each clan consists of people who believe themselves to be descended from a distant common ancestor—that is, they consider themselves to be related. Each clan has a *totem*—an object in natural life which, (a bit like the tartans of Scottish clans) Arunta clan members believe to be special to them. In fact, the totem is so special for them that, according to Durkheim, they imbue it with a *religious* significance. On rare but important occasions the whole of the clan (including members of many different bands, of course) will gather as a group to worship the totem. In addition, during their day-to-day lives as band members, whenever they come across their particular totem, they will treat it with reverence—as a kind of *sacred* object.

How should we explain this? Employing the assumptions of functionalist theory, Durkheim is not interested in any *intentions* of particular Arunta individuals to have totemism in their society. After all, it was present among them before they were born and will continue to be there after they die. He wants instead to identify the *function* totemism performs for the Arunta social system. The answer he gives is this.

Living such a precarious life (without things we take for granted like hospitals or welfare institutions) the Arunta people above all need *each other* to survive. The groups to which the Arunta belong are their lifeline; the obligations other humans feel to help them when they need it are their only hope. In these circumstances, argues Durkheim, what is needed is some means of ensuring the group *remains* important in the eyes of Arunta individuals. Furthermore, the recognition of the obligations must extend beyond band members alone. If not, all that would happen (as it does so often between peoples who feel no obligations towards one another) would be that individual bands would compete—and fight—for the limited resources available in their world. They would soon wipe each other out.

The answer to this problem of the need for the integration of the separate groups which make up the Arunta social system is *Totemism*. The totem is, as Durkheim puts it, *"the flag of the clan"*. It is a *symbol* of those people in Arunta society with whom band members do not live, but who they know look upon them as relatives. They are special people who should be helped and supported whenever necessary. Because of the totem, the group's symbol, its members are reminded of its existence when they might otherwise forget. On the ceremonial occasions when the whole group gathers to worship the totem, there takes place a collective reaffirmation of its importance to them. As Durkheim puts it, by worshipping the totem, the Arunta are really worshipping the group.

The *function* of totemism, then, is to *integrate* the Arunta social system (to draw its parts together and sustain it as a whole). It is, in Durkheim's terms, an instrument of *social solidarity*. Clearly, totemism is here being explained not in terms of what it *is*—what the content of its doctrines or beliefs are—but what it *does,* that is, the function it performs for the social system. Functionalists since Durkheim's time have extended this analysis to all religions. For them, religion must always exist, since all social systems need integrating. They argue that what is interesting is not what is *different* about the beliefs and rituals characteristic of, say, Totemism, Buddhism, Hinduism, Judaism, Protestantism and Catholicism. For them, what is interesting is what is *similar* about what they each *do*—about the *integrative functions* all these religions perform for their social systems.

In recent times, of course, functionalists have been faced with the rather tricky problem of explaining how something as apparently essential for the continuance of society could have become so unimportant in so many of them. Undeterred, some have argued that even though religion has apparently lost importance in many societies (a process known as secularisation), the function of integration continues to be performed, by present-day functional *equivalents* of religion. Thus some theorists have claimed that this happens even in anti-religious societies such as some communist countries. Commitment to communist ideas, and the holding of national rituals, like the May Day parades in the Soviet Union, are said to be equivalent to religion. They meet the same needs for a shared set of values and the performance of collective rituals which more orthodox religious beliefs and practices meet in other societies.

Even in highly secularised western societies some functionalists have seen a new kind of religion performing ancient functions. Robert Bellah argues for the existence of a 'Civil Religion' in the U.S.A., in which American history and institutions are utilised to ensure the reaffirmation of essential American values and sentiments. As Roy Wallis puts it: "Bellah finds evidence for the existence of civil religion in such events as Presidential Inaugurations. Inaugural addresses tend to be couched in a religious idiom, referring to God in general terms and to the travails of America as a modern Israel led out of Egypt. This stylised rhetoric is taken as indicating a real commitment on the part of participants to symbols and values which unify and integrate the community and provide sacred legitimation for its affairs. Other more frequent ceremonials such as Thanksgiving Day and Memorial Day are similarly held to integrate families into the civil religion, or to unify the community around its values."

To repeat, what is very apparent here is an interest in the *effects* of a religion rather than its constituent beliefs. First, many different kinds of religious belief-systems are lumped together because of the similar integrative function they all perform. Second, very different kinds of belief-systems altogether, without any reference to, for example, Gods or spirits or an after life, are nevertheless thought of as equivalent to religion. Again this is because of the similar function they are seen as performing. This also directs our attention to a related principal characteristic of functionalist explanation. Clearly, the inhabitants of India or Ireland or Israel would argue that their religions are not similar at all, since their focus would be on the beliefs themselves, not their effects. For the functionalist, however, the explanation of a belief or a pattern of behaviour observable in a society held by the *members* of that society is not usually thought to be particularly relevant. For them what needs to be identified are the often *un*intended consequences of people's actions and beliefs—those consequences which, though not necessarily apparent to the people concerned, nevertheless have crucial functional effects for the social system. To distinguish between these two levels of analysis, functionalists generally refer to the 'manifest' functions of institutions—those of which people are aware—and their 'latent' functions—those of which people are often *un*aware. These latent functions are no less important to identify in order to understand the functioning and persistence of social systems.

These, then, are the characteristic features of functional analysis.
1   An interest in the *effect* of an activity or belief rather than its constituent *ingredients* i.e. what it *does* rather than what it *is*;
2   A stress on the need to often go beyond peoples' own explanations for their activities in order to reveal the true functional significance of institutionalised behaviour and belief.

By looking at a couple of famous examples from functionalist anthropology we will be able to clearly see the character and consequences of these intrinsic functionalist interests.

The Kula

Bronislaw Malinowski was the first anthropologist to undertake a long-term piece of field research. For four years (between 1915 and 1918), he lived among the Trobriand Islanders, who inhabit a group of tiny coral islands off the coast of New Guinea. He published a number of books describing and explaining various aspects of Trobriand life, but the most

Functionalism

famous is *Argonauts of the Western Pacific*. This is an account of an elaborate gift exchange institution called the Kula, which is carried on by the Trobrianders among themselves and with the members of other tribal societies who live on surrounding islands. Malinowski described the Kula as follows: "The Kula is a form of exchange, of extensive, inter-tribal character; it is carried on by communities inhabiting a wide ring of islands which form a closed circuit ... Along this route, articles of the two kinds, and these two kinds only, are constantly travelling in opposite directions. In the directions of the hands of a clock, moves constantly one of these kinds—long necklaces of red shell, called *soulava*. In the opposite direction moves the other kind—bracelets of white shell called *mwali*. Each of these two articles as it travels in its own direction on the closed circuit, meets on its way articles of the other class and is constantly being exchanged for them. Every movement of the Kula articles, every detail of the transactions is fixed and regulated by a set of traditional rules and conventions, and some acts of the Kula are accompanied by an elaborate magical ritual and public ceremonies.

On every island and in every village, a more or less limited number of men take part in the Kula—that is to say, receive the goods, hold them for a short time, and then pass them on. Therefore every man who is in the Kula, periodically though not regularly, receives one of several mwali (arm-shells), or a soulava necklace (necklace of red shell disks), and then has to hand it on to one of his partners, from whom he receives the opposite commodity in exchange. Thus no man ever keeps any of the articles for any length of time in his possession. One transaction does not finish the Kula relationship, the rule being 'once in the Kula, always in the Kula', and a partnership between two men is a permanent and lifelong affair. Again, any given mwali or soulava may always be found travelling and changing hands, and there is no question of its ever settling down, so that the principle 'once in the Kula, always in the Kula' applies also to the valuables themselves."

How is such an institution to be explained? Malinowski argues that from the point of view of those involved in it, the Kula is a significant way of gaining *prestige*. In industrial society things are used in order to gain prestige too, of course. Thorstein Veblen coined the famous phrase 'conspicuous consumption' to describe the way people in Western societies do not simply own things for the practical uses they have—their *utility* value. He points out how we also seek to own things for the value they have for us as *symbols* of who we would like others to think we are. Though there might be a certain utility advantage for the Rolls Royce owner in terms of the extra comfort the car affords him or her, at least as important is its value as a *status symbol*. It symbolises or expresses the resources, and, by implication, the importance, of its owner. The same goes for the possession of mink coats, diamonds, enormous houses in particular residential areas etc. etc.

The Kula valuables similarly enable Trobrianders and their neighbours to gain prestige. But they do so in a rather different way from the way our valuables do for us. In the Kula there is no advantage or prestige attached to *keeping* a valuable. You receive the admiration of others for two reasons. First because *you* were chosen by your partner to be the recipient of the valuable article rather than any other of his partners. Second because you can show yourself to be generous by *giving it away* again in turn. As Malinowski puts it: "Ownership ... in (the) Kula, is quite a special economic relation. A man who is in the Kula never keeps any article for longer than, say, a year or two. Even this exposes him to the reproach of being niggardly ... on the other hand, each man has an enormous number of articles passing through his hands during his lifetime, of which he enjoys a temporary possession, and which he keeps in trust for a time. The possession hardly ever makes him use the articles, and he remains under the obligation soon again to hand them on to one of his partners. But the temporary ownership allows him to draw a great deal of renown, to exhibit his article, to tell how he obtained it, and to plan to whom he is going to give it."

Here, then, social honour is not attached to the acquisition in order to *possess*. The purpose of wanting to acquire is not to own, but to give *away* again. In Malinowski's words: "... a man who owns a thing is naturally expected to share it, to distribute it, to be its trustee and dispenser ... the main symptom of being powerful is to be wealthy and of wealth is to be generous ... the more important he is, the more will he desire to shine by his generosity ..."

It would appear that here we have the answer to the Kula. It is a system of 'conspicuous generosity', to parody Veblen. It is a way of allowing people to gain importance and to be seen to be important. Status-seeking is not the prerogative of the materialist West. The Trobrianders wish to be thought of as important and powerful too—they just use different ways to do it. From the point of view of individual Trobrianders this *is* almost certainly the whole story. For them it is an institution geared to the pursuit of status. But is their story the only one about the Kula that needs to be told? After all, they *learnt* to Kula; it existed before they did. Since they did not invent it can we rely only on *their* views of what it is about? The functionalist in Malinowski will not allow him to stop at the actors' explanations of their activities. He also wants to know why the Kula is necessary for the Trobriand social system. He wants to know what the Kula *does*—what its *function* is.

Functionalism

The answers Malinowski and later functionalist analysts of his material give run along these lines. Because many of the Kula exchanges take place between partners who live on islands many miles apart, its existence allows economic and political relationships to take place between people who would otherwise never meet. The result is a greater economic and political integration of the whole of Trobriand society and of different societies with each other than would otherwise have been possible.

The economic function of the Kula

Though Kula partners are not allowed to engage in ordinary trading with one another, non-partners are. Thus an expedition of a large number of members of one island to others will not simply result in Kula exchanges. Between men who are not Kula partners, bartering for non-Kula goods is quite normal. According to Malinowski, this is an important *latent* function of the Kula. It makes possible trading relations between people who would otherwise never come into contact with one another, for their mutual economic benefit. "... side by side with the ritual exchange of arm-shells and necklaces, the natives carry on ordinary trade, bartering from one island to another a great number of utilities, often improcurable in the district to which they are imported and indispensable there."

Here, then, is an economic function of the Kula of which its members would be either unaware or certainly consider of secondary importance to the Kula exchanges. In contrast, for functionalists, it is such *un*intended consequences of people's activities which are usually of the greatest importance to identify.

The political function of the Kula

It is the fact that the Kula makes possible such long-distance social interaction, embracing the whole of Trobriand society and linking the Trobrianders with more distant tribal societies, that functionalists have usually pounced on as its key. Two excerpts from the Argonauts give a flavour of its political function which Malinowski himself identifies. "An average man has a few partners near by ... and with these partners he is generally on very friendly terms ... the overseas partner is, on the other hand, a host, patron and ally in a land of danger and insecurity."

"The Kula is thus an extremely big and complex institution ... It welds together a considerable number of tribes, and it embraces a vast complex of activities, inter-connected and playing into one another, so as to form one organic whole."

Both Malinowski's functionalism and the integrative consequences of the Kula he sees as so central to its significance, are clearly apparent here. In a more recent re-study of Malinowski's data (1962) J. Singh Uberoi argues that the integrative function of the Kula is even more fundamental than Malinowski himself acknowledged. His thesis is this. Only Kula objects among valuable things are owned by individuals rather than by groups of kin. Only in the Kula do people enter into relations as individuals rather than as representatives of their kin-groups. Only in the Kula is self-interest rather than group-interest the motivating force.

How does this reduction in the importance of kinship relations in the Kula allow it to enable a great political *integration* of the whole community? Uberoi argues that because the Kula enables people to be released from their obligations to their kin groups they are better able to perceive of Trobriand society as a wider whole. Rather in the way the totem tells the Arunta about the wider society on which they ultimately depend, the Kula encourages the Trobriander to think of their society as a whole, rather than as a collection of competing kin groups. This is how Uberoi puts it: "... the Kula extends the political society beyond the district by periodically depreciating the ties which bind an individual to the other members of his own local lineage or district, and re-emphasising his obligations towards his Kula partner, who belongs to an otherwise opposed district ... on a Kula expedition ... each individual ... stands by and for himself, released from the normal restraints of group solidarity; but because he pursues his individual self-interest through wooing his Kula partner, he stands not only for himself, but also for the whole chain of partners which goes to make up the Kula ring ..." the Kula valuables symbolise to "the normally kin-bound individuals ... the highest point of their individual self-interest" and also "the interest of the widest political association of which they all partake"—the Kula.

This is a typical functionalist analysis. The accounts of their activities by the people involved in them are forgotten. The interest is in what *good* an institutionalised activity is doing for the society as a whole. The assumption is that an institution would not exist unless it was necessary. The observer's job is to see *why* it is necessary, what *function* it is performing. The Trobriander sails to distant islands to pursue his self-interest and to maximise his prestige. Unbeknown to him, but glaringly apparent to the perceptive functionalist, what he is *really* doing is integrating his society, both economically and politically.

We can look at another famous example of gift exchange to underline these characteristics of functionalist analysis. Here too the actors' motives are self-interested. Indeed, in this case it is sometimes the pursuit of self-interest at the deliberate expense of people you see as your rivals. Yet, even in the midst of such self-confessed conflict, the functionalist will find goodness and benefit for the social system in which these competitors live.

The Potlatch

The Potlatch is a form of gift exchange found among the Indian peoples who live along the coastal regions of North-west America and Canada. The following is an account of the institution in its original form, before western influences modified its character somewhat.

In these Indian societies different families occupied various positions on a hierarchy or ladder of prestige. The way prestige—and a place on the ladder—was acquired was by the use of potlatches. A potlatch was a feast or party at which the host distributed gifts to the guests. Originally the potlatch gifts were largely consumable items, like meat, fat and skins. The purpose of this was to be seen to be generous. For these Indians, as for the Trobrianders, generosity was the principal way of acquiring social honour and public admiration. As an early authority on the potlatch, H.G. Barnett, puts it: "... virtue rested in publicly disposing of wealth, not in its mere acquisition and accumulation. Accumulation in any quantity by borrowing or otherwise was, in fact, unthinkable unless it be for the purposes of an immediate redistribution."

The degree of generosity required of the host depended on the position in the hierarchy he aspired to. Usually this was the position his family had traditionally held. Thus, members of the most important families were expected to hold the grandest potlatches at which the greatest generosity by the hosts would be shown. Less important families held less generous potlatches and so on. Once a claim to a social position had been made by the exhibition of appropriate generosity at someone's first potlatch, subsequent potlatches were designed to reaffirm the holder's right to this position.

Although the holding of a potlatch did not validate the claim of the host, among most Indian tribes claims were accepted without disagreement. In effect, potlatches were vehicles for confirming publicly accepted facts already conceded by the community at large.

Among one of these tribes however—the Kwakiutl, who lived on Vancouver Island—this form of ceremonial gift exchange was far from being so peaceful. It became the context in which a fierce competition for prestige and social status took place. It is this competitive form of potlatching that has had most publicity, gaining notoriety from the accounts of such as Ruth Benedict (*Patterns of Culture*) and Helen Codere (*Fighting with Property*).

As among other Indian tribes, the grandest potlatches were held by Kwakiutl tribal chiefs. This is how Marvin Harris describes their characteristic features. "The Kwakiutl used to live in plank-house villages set close to the shore in the midst of cedar and fir rain forests. They fished and hunted along the island-studded sounds and fiords of Vancouver in huge dugout canoes ...

A Kwakiutl chief was never content with the amount of respect he was getting from his own followers and from neighbouring chiefs. He was always insecure about his status. True enough, the family titles to which he laid claim belonged to his ancestors. But there were other people who could trace descent from the same ancestors and who were entitled to vie with him for recognition as a chief. Every chief therefore felt the obligation to justify and validate his chiefly pretensions. The prescribed manner for doing this was to hold potlatches. Each potlatch was given by a host chief and his followers to a guest chief and his followers. The object of the potlatch was to show that the host chief was more truly entitled to chiefly status and that he was more exalted than the guest chief. To prove this point, the host chief gave the rival chief and his followers quantities of valuable gifts. The guests would belittle what they had received and vow to hold a return potlatch at which their own chief would prove that he was greater than the former host by giving back even larger quantities of more valuable gifts.

Preparations for potlatch required the accumulation of fresh and dried fish, fish oil, berries, animal skins, blankets, and other valuables. On the appointed day, the guests paddled up to the host village and went into the chief's house ...

The host chief and his followers arranged in neat piles the wealth that was to be given away. The visitors stared at their host sullenly as he pranced up and down, boasting about how much he was about to give them. As he counted out the boxes of fish oil, baskets full of berries, and piles of blankets, he commented derisively on the poverty of his rivals. Laden with gifts, the guests finally were free to paddle back to their own village. Stung to the quick, the guest chief and his followers vowed to get even. This could only be achieved by inviting their rivals to a return potlatch and obliging them to accept even greater amounts of valuables than they had given away ... potlatch stimulated a ceaseless flow of prestige and valuables moving in opposite directions.

An ambitious chief and his followers had potlatch rivals in several different villages at once. Specialists in counting property kept track of what had to be done in each village in order to even the scores. If a chief managed to get the better of his rivals in one place, he still had to confront his adversaries in another ...

... At some potlatches blankets and other valuables were not given away but were destroyed. Sometimes successful potlatch chiefs decided to hold 'grease feasts' at which boxes of oil obtained from candlefish were poured on the fire in the centre of the house. As the flames roared up dark grease smoke filled the room. The guests sat impassively or even complained about the chill in the air ... At some grease feasts the flames ignited the planks in the roof and an entire house would become a potlatch offering, causing the greatest shame to the guests and much rejoicing among the hosts."

How should such apparently bizarre behaviour be explained? Ruth Benedict sees it as "unabashed megalomania". For her it is simply a case of an obsessive desire for greater power and prestige than their rivals, driving chiefs to produce more and more—though not for their *own* consumption, of course. Glory lay in giving away what had been accumulated; humiliation lay in having to receive it. The impoverished producer triumphed; the richly-laden consumer was defeated. He who had nothing had everything; he who had everything had nothing.

Benedict's analysis is clearly one with which the Kwakiutl themselves would agree. But as usual, an analysis of an institution which coincides with the view of it held by its practitioners is, for functionalists, likely to be at best partial, and at worst plain wrong. The question they want answering is: What is the function of the potlatch for the Kwakiutl social system? As with the Kula, knowing what the potlatch *is* is not enough. What does it *do?* According to Marvin Harris, the most important function the potlatch performs is an economic one. He argues that institutions like the potlatch—competitive feasting institutions—are always found in certain kinds of society. These are societies which do not have a government or ruler with sufficient power to make decisions. Such societies are called 'stateless' societies. It is not that all stateless societies will exhibit competitive feasting but that where competitive feasting exists, it will be in a stateless society. This is because of the function such an institution performs for such a society. This is Harris' argument, again a clear example of functionalist thinking.

All societies need some mechanism whereby goods are produced and distributed in a way which benefits the whole community. Usually this economic function is performed as part of the duties of a government. Some societies—stateless societies—do not have a government, however. Nevertheless, like all social systems, they still need some means of ensuring all their members benefit from economic activity. In effect, to use functionalist jargon, there must be a 'functional equivalent' of a government in stateless societies to ensure this happens.

Harris argues that competitive feasting—of which the potlatch among the Kwakiutl is the most famous example in anthropology—is such a functionally equivalent mechanism in many stateless societies. The chiefs among the Kwakiutl had no overall power. They led only their local tribes. Despite this, the Kwakiutl social system as a whole needed a distribution of goods which benefitted everyone who lived in it. This was particularly important in the case of the Kwakiutl, because the production of foodstuffs fluctuated seasonally between areas on Vancouver Island. At some times of the year some tribal areas would be abundant with food, while in other areas people went hungry. At other times this situation was reversed.

Clearly, says Harris, the Kwakiutl social system needed an institution to function to enable the redistribution of food from abundant areas to impoverished areas. The potlatch, he argues, was this institution. Chiefs only held feasts for their opponents when they knew they could lay on a huge range of consumable gifts for their guests—when food was abundant. Their motive was self-interest—to be seen to be as generous as possible. But, says Harris, a by-product of this pursuit of self-interest meant that the necessary economic function would be performed. The hardest-hit tribes at any time would *automatically* be the visitors while the best-off would *automatically* be the hosts.

In this way, says Harris, despite the lack of a government and despite fluctuations in production from time to time and from place to place, the potlatch functioned to ensure an equal distribution of food among the Kwakiutl society as a whole.

In Harris' explanations the characteristic features of functionalist analysis are once again clearly exhibited. If something exists in a social system it must be performing a function—it must be doing some good. Even though the particular institution here—the potlatch—appears to be a recipe for prolonged conflict and competition between tribal groups, and even though the participants in it see the institution this way themselves, it is in fact no such thing. The Kwakiutl hold potlatches for the pursuit of prestige, to gain a victory over an opponent by generosity. For Harris the functionalist, what they are really doing is ensuring economic prosperity for all. The Kwakiutl encounter the Potlatch as an

Functionalism

integral part of their culture upon being born. They learn how important it is through socialisation. Though they are learning one cultural story about its significance whereas the reality is in fact another, the end result is the same—the social system benefits. As in all societies, the Kwakiutl learn to *want* to do what they *have* to do to ensure the survival of their society.

Functionalism has exerted a tremendous influence on sociology. As we noted at the beginning of the chapter, for much of the first half of this century it occupied a largely unchallenged theoretical position in the subject. Through the influence of anthropology in Britain and of functionalism's High Priest, Talcott Parsons, and his supporters in America, by the middle of the century sociology came to be more or less synonymous with functionalist sociology. Other theoretical approaches were kept well in the background. The sociological enterprise was seen as principally concerned with a search for the 'real' significance of social institutions—the contribution they make to the maintenance of the social systems in which they are found. Because its influence has substantially waned today, it is easy to be over-critical of the rather narrow vision of functionalism's adherents. Now it seems rather strange that during functionalism's ascendancy so little attention should have been paid to relations of dominance and subordination, advantage and disadvantage in society. It also seems self-evident that humans must be recognised to be more than just 'cultural dopes', obediently learning sets of cultural prescriptions for action so that their social systems can persist. Today it seems clear that sociology must take account of the interpretive abilities of people in order to properly understand their actions.

In our eagerness to demonstrate the errors and partialities in functionalism/structural-consensus theory, we must not forget to acknowledge the contribution this kind of theory has made to sociology. The unintended social consequences of people's beliefs and actions *are* important to recognise. Sociology *does* have an important revelatory task. It *is* necessary to sometimes go beyond people's own explanations for their actions in order to properly understand social behaviour. This is undoubtedly functionalism's contribution. Nevertheless, we would also be quite wrong to deny functionalism's weaknesses. Four main ones are usually identified. It is argued that functionalism

i   has an inherent tendency to 'reify' society.
ii   is not able to adequately explain social change.
iii   is based upon an oversocialised view of human beings.
iv   does not take enough account of power and conflict in society.

Functionalism and the 'reification' of society

Functionalists explain the existence of institutionalised patterns of behaviour and belief in terms of the good effects these have for the social system in which they are found. Institutions are not the product of decisions made by individuals since they exist prior to these individuals. The problem of social order is not how human beings can create an ordered society. It is how social systems can create social beings socialised into conforming to institutionalised rules of behaviour necessary for their persistence. This insistence that societies acquire their functioning characteristics prior to the existence of their members leaves a rather awkward question, however. If *people* do not decide what is functional for their society, then who *does* decide? The functionalist seems to be left with the proposition that the social system itself decides what is good for it. Yet this is clearly absurd. Societies cannot think, only people can. This is known as the problem of "reification". Functionalists seem to "reify" society—to treat it as a thing—by endowing it with the ability to think and act intentionally that actually only humans have.

Functionalism and social change

Functionalism seems to promote a static and conservative picture of society. The functionalist position is that institutions continue to exist because they are functional—they are satisfying a need of the social system. The job of the sociologist is to reveal what the good effects of particular institutions are. This seems to come remarkably close to *automatically* justifying what the status quo in a particular society happens to be. At bottom this seems to imply that all persisting social arrangements in a society *must* be beneficial otherwise they would not remain in existence. The problem with this is not just that it denies the *desirability* of social change. It also leaves the functionalist unable to explain the fact that social change does take place a lot of the time. As John Rex puts it: "... All forms of functionalist theory as it is usually understood are logically debarred from being able to put forward any sociological theory of change. This is because the whole functionalist effort is devoted to showing why things are as they are. They are as they are because they are demanded by the needs of the social structure."

The other two criticisms of functionalism—that it is based upon an over-socialised view of human beings and that it fails to take account of power and conflict in society—bring us into the realm of mainstream theoretical debates in sociology with which this book is concerned.

Functionalism and socialisation

As we said in Chapter 1, *interpretive* theories have crucial objections to the functionalist/structural-consensus model. For them, the real criticism of functionalism is that it over-emphasises socialisation as an explanation of social behaviour. The interpretive case is that people are not passive recipients of cultural recipes for social action. Among living things humans alone are able to *choose* how to act. Far from being a simple reflection of cultural prescription, such choices are made in the light of how people see the world—particularly how they interpret the actions of others. Social action is thus *voluntary* action. It is action chosen in the light of the actor's interpretation of reality.

Functionalism, power and conflict

As we also saw in Chapter 1, the criticism *structural-conflict* theory makes of the functionalist/consensus approach to social life has two elements. First, according to conflict theory, functionalism fails to take account of the influence on behaviour of society's structures of inequality. The argument here is that people are not only influenced by the norms and values of the culture into which they are socialised. Their social lives are also crucially influenced by the advantages they possess; there are practical, as well as normative, constraints on behaviour which bring the advantaged and the disadvantaged into conflict. Second, for conflict theorists, functionalism is based on a fundamentally flawed conception of the role of socialisation into cultural rules. In conflict theory, norms and values only have the character they do because their role is to obscure, as well as to legitimate, the facts of inequality in society. Far from socialisation being the instrument of social order and cohesion, it is in fact a mechanism of power and control.

The demise of functionalism

In what follows there is no attempt to provide any insight into the character of the various interpretive or conflict schools of thought that have emerged out of the demise of functionalism. I simply list the main ones and refer to some of their most notable practitioners. The purpose is to allow you to get some idea of the diversity of approaches that can be subsumed under the general headings of interpretivism and conflict theory and to introduce you to some of the more important names working within these traditions. As you do more sociology, the differences between these various schools and their proponents will become clearer.

Though of no real significance for British or American sociology until the 1950's, interpretive and conflict alternatives to functionalism had long been in existence.

Interpretive theories

Interpretive theories have their roots in a strand of German philosophy. *Max Weber* (1864-1920), one of the three great classical sociological theorists (along with Marx and Durkheim), though by no means exclusively an interpretivist, first of all applied this approach to social life in his theory of *'social action'*. His definition of social action clearly bears the interpretive stamp. "In 'action' is included all human behaviour when and in so far as the acting individual attaches a subjective meaning to it ... Action is social in so far as, by virtue of the subjective meaning attached to it by the acting individual (or individuals) it takes account of the behaviour of others and is thereby oriented in its course."

Within the interpretive tradition *phenomenologists* like the Austrian *Alfred Schutz* have developed Weber's work, and pointed the way for the emergence of the most radical interpretive approach to social life—*ethnomethodology*. Ethnomethodologists have been particularly influential in the U.S.A. in recent years; *Harold Garfinkel* is probably the best known figure in American ethnomethodology. Prior to this, the interpretive flag in the U.S.A. was flown principally by *symbolic interactionism*. This theory was developed in the 1920's and 1930's by *George Herbert Mead* but kept largely in the background thereafter by the rise to dominance of Talcott Parsons and functionalism. However, the fall from grace of functionalism in the 1950's and 1960's allowed symbolic interactionism to grow significantly in influence. During the 1960's interactionist writers like *Howard Becker* and *Erving Goffman* produced some of the most stimulating interpretive studies of social life in the literature. Indeed, at this time, the interactionist approach began to be seen by many, particularly in the States, as the answer to the interpretive criticisms of the functionalist view of socialisation and of the relationship between the individual and society. Chapter 4 examines symbolic interactionism, and a closely related approach called labelling theory, in detail and takes a briefer look at ethnomethodology.

Structural-conflict theories

Much conflict theory is derived from the work of *Karl Marx* (1818-1883). His writings have had a huge global political impact during this century of course. Indeed by today, one half of the world is organised on principles that claim to be Marxist.

During this century a number of European writers have attempted, in different ways, to modify and modernise the Marxist model to bring it to terms with developments in the contemporary capitalist world. Some of the most important of these *neo-Marxists* are the Italian *Antonio Gramsci,* the Germans *Jurgen Habermas, Theodore Adorno,* and *Herbert Marcuse,* (members of a neo-Marxist school called *Critical Theory*), the Greek *Nicos Poulantzas* and the Frenchman *Louis Althusser.*

Despite their work, it was not until the demise of functionalism in the 1950's and early 1960's that conflict theory began to make any real impression on sociology in Britain. At this time, through the work of Marxist writers like *Peter Worsley, Ralph Miliband, John Westergaard* and *Perry Anderson* as well as of non-Marxist conflict theorists like *John Rex* and *Ralf Dahrendorf,* a real structuralist alternative to consensus theory/functionalism began to be developed.

Why should it have taken until this time for the conflict approach, and Marxist sociology in particular, to have made its mark on Western sociology? At least some of the answer lies in the experiences of people in the 1960's. This was the decade of social reappraisal. The smug complacency encouraged by the economic prosperity of the 1950's, when the then Prime Minister, Harold Macmillan, could confidently proclaim that his British constituents had "never had it so good" had been replaced by a genuine concern for social justice and a real awareness of inequality and deprivation. Poverty had been 'rediscovered', both in G.B. and the U.S. The Civil Rights movement in America began to demand equality for blacks. The feminist movement began to demand equality for women. U.S.A. imperialism—most notoriously in Vietnam—was denounced by many in the western world.

In such a context, where social change was being demanded and conflict between different groups in society clearly apparent, functionalism began to be seen by many as more and more remote from the real world. As a theory which sets out to explain the benefits of social institutions, to reveal the mechanisms by which social systems achieve cohesion and integration and to show how they persist, it seemed hardly relevant in a world where many had begun to see *dis*advantage and *in*equality, where conflict and a lack of social cohesion were clearly apparent, and where social change seemed necessary. In such circumstances it is not surprising that alongside the emergence of interpretive alternatives to functionalism, another kind of alternative theory, which *does* explain conflict, which *does* confront change, and which *does* attempt to predict the future, should have proved intellectually appealing for many. We will now turn to look at this theory in the next chapter.

3 Marxist theory

In Marxist theory the most important activity of human beings is economic activity—the production of material goods. For the Marxist, "... Mankind must first of all eat, drink, have shelter and clothing, before it can pursue politics, science, art, religion etc." (Engels—speech at Marx's graveside).

According to Marx, understanding the way a society organises its production is the key to understanding the whole of its social structure. The Marxist view is that "... the production of the means of subsistence ... forms the foundation upon which the state institutions, the legal conceptions, art and even the ideas on religion, of the people concerned have been evolved."

Because Marx stresses economic production as the key structural feature of any society he called the way it organises its production its *Infrastructure*. Economic activity, that is, is the *basis* of all else in that society. The rest of its social organisation—its non-economic activities, ideas, beliefs and philosophies—he calls its *Superstructure*. It is easy to see why. The terms are meant to convey the way in which a society's superstructure is determined and created by its infrastructure. One set of activities is built upon, and determined by, another.

For Marx social structures are not randomly created. He argues that there is a quite definite pattern to the way societies in different parts of the world and at different times in history organise their production of material goods. This theory of history and society is called *Historical Materialism*. For our purposes we can identify its following elements.

First, all societies that have existed or do exist today exhibit one of five different ways of organising production. These different ways of producing goods Marx called *Modes of Production*. The five are—in chronological order— the *Primitive Communist, Ancient, Feudal, Capitalist* and *Communist* modes.

Second, apart from the first and last modes of production—the Primitive Communist and Communist modes—each mode of production has one crucial characteristic in common. Each is a way of producing goods based on *Classes*. Though the term 'class' has different uses elsewhere in sociology (and all sorts of uses in commonsense speech) the Marxist usage is quite a specific one. According to Marx, in all non-communist societies—in the Ancient, Feudal and Capitalist modes— there are just two classes that matter. There is the class that *owns* the means of production—it is their *property*—and there is the class that does not own it.

In systems of production based on classes goods are produced in a quite definite way. The majority of people, who do not own the means of production, do the productive work for the benefit of those—the minority—who do own it. In Marxist theory, this is the key feature of non-communist societies at any time in history. The production of material goods (the most important activity of humans, remember) *always* takes place by means of the *exploitation* of the labour of the majority, non-property-owning, class by the minority class who own the means of production and who do not work. That is, the relationship between classes is a *conflict* relationship.

There are no classes in either of the communist modes. In primitive communist societies people cannot produce a surplus. This is usually because of an inhospitable environment or a lack of technological know-how or a combination of the two. Because such peoples only produce enough to allow them to exist at subsistence level, everyone has to work, there is no surplus property and there are therefore no classes. In the communist mode there are no classes because private property has been abolished—people are not able to own the means of production.

Because in any class-based mode of production goods are produced in this exploitative way, in Marxist writing the owners of the means of production are usually called the *dominant* class while the non-owning, exploited class who do the productive work are called the *subordinate* class.

According to Marx, the history of human society is the history of different kinds of productive systems based on class exploitation. He says we can divide up the history of any society into different *epochs* or ages, each of which is dominated by one particular mode of production with its own characteristic class relationships. All societies will eventually pass through all these stages in history and all will eventually become communist. However, not all societies in the world have yet reached the same stage as each other. This is why at any particular time in history different societies exhibit different modes of production—they are at different stages of historical development.

What distinguishes different modes of production from one another? All non-communist modes have in common the production of goods by means of the domination and exploitation of one class by the other. What is different in each case is who the classes are. Each non-communist mode of production has a different, dominant, property-owning class and a different subordinate, exploited, non-property-owning class. Furthermore, each mode grows out of the death of the previous one.

The Ancient Mode of Production

The oldest form of class production—which is why it has its name—is the Ancient mode of production. This mode grew out of the subsistence Primitive Communist mode primarily because of technological improvements. For example, in the Iron Age humans developed productive techniques which allowed specialised animal farming and settled agricultural production. This in turn enabled the production of a surplus and allowed a more complex division of labour than was possible in a purely subsistence economy. In effect, a dominant class of *non*-producers could emerge.

The distinguishing feature of this mode of production is that people are owned as productive property by other, more powerful, people. That is, it is production based on *Slavery*. Here then, the dominant class are *masters* and the subordinate class are their *slaves*. Production takes place by means of the involuntary labour of people who are owned as property by others.

Ancient Greece and Rome provide the classic examples of slavery as a mode of production. In the Greek and Roman empires something in the region of a third of the population were slaves. Most of these had entered into slavery as prisoners of the wars undertaken as part of the Imperialist (empire-building) policies of the Greek and Roman states.

One of the main reasons why the Ancient mode of production disintegrated was that the state power upon which it depended became eroded. As it became more and more difficult for the ancient states to control and coerce people living in parts of their empires often thousands of miles away from their centres, so too did the possibility of sustaining slavery as a mode of production.

The Feudal Mode of Production

In its place emerged a new mode of production of a much more local character called Feudalism. Feudal production was based upon the ability of warriors or nobles controlling small local territories by force of arms to coerce and exploit an agricultural labour force. In Feudalism the dominant class are therefore the controllers of land—the *lords*—and the subordinate class are the *serfs*. Here production takes place by means of the labour of those who *have* to work the land in order to survive. But since these labourers do not own this land but are merely tenants on it, they are obliged to give up much of the product of their labour as rent—

called *tithe*—to the landlords.

Feudalism dominated Europe from the Dark Ages until early modern times. Two factors in particular heralded its death and helped to usher in a new mode of production based on class exploitation. First, strongly centralised political power became re-established in Europe in the form of Absolutist monarchies. This allowed sufficient state control to be exercised within national territories in European countries for proper legal systems to be devised and enforced. This in turn provided the opportunity for economic activity to begin to extend beyond local feudal boundaries and for widespread trade to become possible.

Second, as a result of the changes brought about by the Agricultural Revolution, agricultural production became rationalised and more efficient. One of the most significant consequences of this was the *Enclosures*. These Acts denied the bulk of the agricultural labour-force the subsistence rights over the strips of land they had been entitled to under Feudalism. Replaced by sheep and by non-labour-intensive farming by machines, these labourers were made land*less*. Thrown off the land and with no other means of subsistence than their *labour power,* a *labour market* thus emerged for the first time, with workers forced to sell their labour to *employers* for a *wage*.

The Capitalist Mode of Production

Production took on a new class character. The labour-power of a class of landless labourers—a *proletariat,* as Marxists call them—began to be purchased for a wage by a class of property-owning employers—for whom the Marxist term is the *bourgeoisie*.

So capitalism developed in Britain before industrialisation; it was *agricultural* goods that were first of all produced in a capitalistic way. It was only later, when factories were built and industrial machines were developed, that *industrial* capitalism became established and an *urban* proletariat emerged.

In capitalist society, the bourgeoisie are the dominant class because, like the masters in slave societies and the lords in feudal societies, they own the productive wealth—the means of production.

During the development of capitalism the character of the property in which capitalists have invested their wealth has altered, of course. In the early stages of capitalism, as we have just noted, productive property primarily took the form of *land,* with the proletariat earning wages as agricultural labourers on this land. Later, *industrial* production gave rise to capitalist investment in *factories and machines* with the proletariat earning wages as industrial manual labourers. Still later, capitalism took on the form typical of contemporary industrial capitalism. Today, instead of actually owning and controlling industrial production themselves, the ownership of productive property usually takes the form of *capital investment in stocks and shares*. (Of course, capitalist landowners, and owners and controllers of their own enterprises—especially the smaller ones—still exist in plenty today as well).

Despite these alterations to the nature of property in capitalist society, for Marxists the character of the class relations between the owners of this property and its non-owners is essentially the same as in the earlier class-based modes of production. Though the bourgeoisie do not make goods themselves, because they own the means of production, they will always profit from the difference between the cost to them of the labour of the proletariat and the value of the goods produced by the proletariat's labour power. The important fact is that workers will *always* be paid less than the value of the goods they produce. If this did not happen, the system could not work. This *surplus value* costs the capitalist nothing and is the tangible symbol of the exploitation of the labour-power of the wage-earners by their employers. Though not as obvious as the extraction of tithe by the feudal lord or the ownership of people by slave-owners, it means the relationship between the capitalist and the wage-earner is of exactly the same kind. In Marx's words *"The history of all hitherto existing society is the history of class stuggle."*

Ideological legitimation

There is an obvious question to be asked about this theory, of course. If it is correct, and the history of humankind *is* the history of class exploitation and class conflict and the structure of all class societies *is* inevitably so unequal, then why is it that the disadvantaged in such societies put up with their lot? Why do subordinate classes in different modes of production allow themselves to be exploited? Clearly, a great deal of class exploitation, even today, is sustained by naked force. Particularly in states run by military and/or authoritarian rulers, the exercise of state power in support of capital is usually only too visible. Central and South America offer clear examples. Comparable to this is the fact that the power of slave-owners and feudal lords was a reflection of their possession, and exercise, of brutal instruments of coercion.

But for Marxists, this is not the whole of the story. For them, some of the answer lies elsewhere—in the realm of human life which for functionalists by itself makes up social structures—the cultural or normative world—the world of ideas. In Marxist theory, ideas, beliefs and values perform a very important task in a class society. The production of goods in such societies inevitably promotes gross inequalities between the classes. For such an exploitative system to persist it must either remain unrecognised by those most disadvantaged by it, or they must be persuaded that it is justifiable. According to Marxists the *dominant* ideas, beliefs and values in a class society, which are the ideas there is most agreement about, are not there by chance. They exist to do precisely these jobs. In Marxist language, they act as *ideologies,* propping up a structure which, without such ideological support, would collapse. (The task performed by this Marxist concept of dominant values is therefore very similar to the role functionalists assign to core values. For both theories, there is inevitably a set of prevailing beliefs in all societies which serve to perpetuate them. The crucial difference concerns the character of the structures thus supported, of course.)

In the Marxist view, a class society's *superstructure* is indispensable to its survival. It represents the society's cultural characteristics and the institutions that promote these characteristics. Its *infrastructure*—its class-based mode of production—only survives so long as the reality of its class character remains unrecognised, or is considered legitimate, by those whom it subordinates. The superstructure ensures this happens.

Marxists therefore argue that although from time to time dominant classes *do* have to resort to naked force to maintain their power and supremacy, the absence of such obvious coercion should not be taken to signify an absence of exploitation. On the contrary, they suggest, all a lack of naked oppression can ever indicate is a lack of opposition, and the lack of any need to use force. It does not mean that domination is not taking place. It is only that the dominated are unaware of their condition, because of the effectiveness of the ideologies into which they have been socialised.

How do such dominant ideas gain such general acceptance? Here again, Marxists would agree with functionalists. Both theories would accept that particular ideas come to prevail through various key agencies of socialisation. In contemporary society, for example, they would both point to the important role played by institutions like the family, the education system and the mass media in promoting generally-held beliefs and values. The essential difference between them concerns their respective interpretations of the *role* of the socialisation process such institutions ensure. For functionalists it is the way we learn those ideas

Marxist theory

we need to know in order to think and behave in ways required of us by the social system. For Marxists it is the way we learn those ideas which serve to hide from our eyes, or to justify, the real character of a class society. For both theories there *is* a prevailing culture which people learn through socialisation. The different between them concerns the job this culture does. For functionalists it ensures social integration. For Marxists it ensures social inequality and domination. This is the key element in the Marxist approach to the superstructure—a society's non-economic institutions and the ideas and beliefs they promote. The assumption is that they exist to prop up a class-based mode of production. The sociologist's task is to analyse this role.

We can look at some prevailing ideas in contemporary capitalist Britain to see how a Marxist would explain their superstructural significance. From the Marxist viewpoint, any ideas in Britain which, for example:
i   divert people's attentions away from the reality of class inequality
ii reproduce demand for goods by encouraging consumerism
iii encourage the wage-earning class to accept their subordinate role
iv justify the inequality between the classes
are assisting to perpetuate capitalism in this society. How is this done? How do such ideas come to prevail? A Marxist approach to the superstructure of contemporary Britain might go along these lines.

1 Diversionary institutions

Capitalist production is exploitative, according to Marxists. A major reason for its survival is that institutions exist to divert the attention of the exploited away from the reality of their condition. One important vehicle doing this is the *Entertainment Industry*. For example, much *popular music* with its characteristic emphasis on the attractions of romantic love and/or sexual satisfaction as the pinnacle of human fulfilment hardly aims to shed light on the reality of class exploitation! Neither does a lot of *popular literature,* though not only by an emphasis on sex/love. Also high on the list of fictional priorities is escapism of other kinds. The never ending production of gangster/detective novels, war novels, science fiction and so on bears testimony to this preoccupation. A substantial proportion of *T.V. and radio programmes* have similar consequences. From situation-comedies to quiz games, from soap opera to cops and robbers, a significant consequence of such T.V. and radio entertainment is that it promotes a trivialisation of reality.

Programmes like these create 'pretend' worlds, where the facts of life in a class society are ignored.

The *family* can also perform a similar task. A dominant belief in contemporary society is that individual emotional satisfaction can only be found in marriage and in child production and rearing. However pleasant or otherwise the successful accomplishment of such goals may be, we must realise that the pursuit of such an achievement renders a desire for fulfilment through other activities, like work, less likely. The result is that exploited, meaningless work is tolerated. Life becomes about the achievement of marital and parental satisfaction in order to compensate. As a Ford car worker told Huw Beynon "I just close my eyes, stick it out and think of the wife and kids."

Finally, much of the *news media* typically perform an important diversionary role in capitalist society too. For example, tabloid newspapers like the *Sun,* the *Star* and the *Mirror, the Mail* and *the Express,* traditionally concentrate on the trivial, the sensational and the titillating rather than on a serious reporting of events. This *deliberate* suppression and distortion of reality can only further encourage people living in a capitalist society to divert their gaze away from inequality, deprivation and exploitation. Indeed, since it is only through mass media that we gain most of our information about reality, a failure to provide such information is not only diversionary. It also means we are being provided with a picture of the world that is false.

2 Consumerism: the reproduction of demand

Capitalism depends upon the reproduction of demand. Any social institution which promotes the purchase of goods perpetuates their production by capitalist means. Clearly, the main way in which we are encouraged to consume is by means of *advertising*. Whether on T.V. and radio or in the cinema, in newspapers and magazines or on bill-boards, such advertisements glorify the possession of material goods (compare this with the values underpinning the Kula and the Potlatch) and thereby promote their acquisition.

The *family* helps reproduce demand too. We normally live in nuclear families—the smallest kind of family unit. Each family is economically independent, purchasing its own goods. This ensures that demand is maximised. Clearly, if we lived in larger households, demand for consumer goods would decrease.

3 The acquiescence of wage-earners in their subordination

Capitalism depends upon the bulk of the population being socialised into accepting a subordinate role. Once again, the *family* plays an important part. It is in the family that we first learn the meaning of authority and obedience. Learning to submit to the wishes of parents provides just the training necessary to cope with being a wage-earner and under the authority of an employer. *Education* obviously reinforces this training.

4 The justification of inequality

Capitalism depends upon its inherent inequalities, if recognised, being accepted as just. It is in *the classroom* that we first encounter both the inevitablity and the justice of inequality. Here we learn that people do not just possess *different* abilities. They possess *better* or *worse* abilities. 'Clever' children succeed and are rewarded with good grades and exam results. 'Less able' children deserve poorer rewards. What better training for life in a society where different abilities are also judged as superior and inferior and judged accordingly? Experiences in school can only encourage people to believe that inequality of reward is just. Such beliefs are expressed in such commonly-held views as these: "Of course doctors should be paid more than dustmen. They do a much more important job." The unequal distribution of rewards among different occupations reflects their importance. Or again "Anyone could be a dustman. Only able/intelligent/skilled people can become doctors". Achievement within an unequal world reflects merit.

In a fundamental way, then, education, with its intrinsic emphasis on competition and selection, on success and failure, on merit and de-merit, teaches members of a capitalist society the justice of inequality. In particular, it teaches the 'less able'—the 'failures'—to expect, and accept, low rewards in their lives. As Frank Parkin puts it: "It has ... sometimes been suggested that the secondary modern system* performs a useful and humane function in psychologically preparing future members of the underclass for the harsh realities of the world awaiting them outside the school gates. However this may be, such a process also has political implications in so far as it encourages the future underclass in the art of accommodating to low status. The more successful the

---

*More usually today, the lower streams in a comprehensive school.

education system is in doing this the more difficult becomes the task of radical groups in encouraging the disprivileged to reject their low status."

Along with other kinds of conflict theorists, Marxist theorists argue that institutions like *education* and, in particular, the *mass media,* justify inequality in another way too. By means of such agencies, stereotypical images of superiority and inferiority, coinciding with class position, gain wide currency. The cultural attributes of the upper class are defined as superior while those of the working class are denigrated. At first glance, these images just seem a bit of fun. There is an identifiable *upper class stereotype* we can all make jokes about. Among other things it is associated with a particular

demeanor	—a lofty disdain for all ordinary mortals and a complete ignorance of the meaning of the word 'self-doubt'.
mode of dress	—in upper-class watering-holes this often involves, among males, what Ralf Dahrendorf has called a kind of 'cultivated dishevellment'. Typically it includes very old baggy cords or cavalry twill trousers; noisy shoes; tweed jackets—old—with patches on the elbows; check shirts (Viyella) and cravats. Green wellies, body warmers and Range Rovers are essential outdoor pieces of equipment as are, for the ladies, tweed skirts and liberty-print headscarves.
manners	—described by Nancy Mitford as 'U' as opposed to 'non-U'.
language	—usually known as the 'O.K. yah' mode of speech. In his novel *The Rachel Papers,* Martin Amis captures this nicely. "The doors opened. A tall ginger-haired boy in green tweed moved gracefully down the steps. He looked at me as if I were a gang of skinheads: not with fear (because the fellows are quite tractable really) but with disapproval. Behind him at a trot came two lantern-jawed girls, calling 'Jamie ... *Jamie'.* Jamie swivelled elegantly. 'Angelica, I'm not going to the Imbenkment. Gregory shall have to take you'. 'But Gregory's in Scotland' one said. 'I can't help thet'. The ginger boy disappeared into an old-fashioned sports car.

Marxist theory

> The students were pouring out steadily now. Each and every one of them was shouting.
> 'Casper, yah, Ormonde Gate, not possible, super, Freddie, five o'clock, *rather,* tea? Bubble, later, race you there, beast, at Oswald's? Double-parked Alfa Romeos, Morgans and M.G.'s jostled and revved ... "

names	—Charles, Simon, Justin, Piers, William, Edward, Gervase, George, Humphrey, Giles; Caroline, Georgina, Harriet, Miranda, Victoria, Alexandra, Clarissa, Felicity.
leisure pursuits	—'horsey' activities—e.g. eventing, trials, point-to-point, flat racing—rugby, lacrosse, cricket.

We could compile a much longer list of both attributes and examples of these attributes but this gives a sufficient flavour of the type. The point is that it stands in direct opposition to stereotypical working-class attributes which, by definition, are 'common', 'vulgar', 'cheap and nasty', etc. in comparison. Working-class people, so the image has it, 'don't know' how to dress and are in particular prone to ghastly clashes of colour or, worse, checks. Neither do they know what or how to eat, spending most of their time shovelling platefuls of fish and chips into their mouths with or without the assistance of cutlery. Their language is common, ungrammatical and mispronounced. They all speak with vulgar accents like Welsh, Scottish, Irish, Yorkshire, Lancashire, East or South (Sarf) London, Birmingham, rustic agricultural etc. etc.—any accent not associated with upper class Home Counties in fact. Working class people play sport—like soccer, snooker and darts—so long as it is associated with the ingestion of enormous quantities of draught beer. Young working class males are called Wayne, Darren, Clint, Floyd and Duane, while working class girls are called Sharon, Tracey, Maureen and Shirley. As they get older working class males are called Bert, Sid, Les, Harry, Stan, Eric, or Ernie. Older working class women are called Dolly, Eedie, Rose, Lizzie, Annie, Gert, Daisy and Florrie. Working class people decorate their homes in gaudy wallpaper and even gaudier furniture, have pictures of African animals or a near-blue Polynesian beauty on their walls, have multifarious ornaments dotted everywhere and the television on all the time. They holiday in Blackpool, Benidorm, Lloret or Butlins.

At first glance the currency of such stereotypes seems harmless enough. Both can be laughed at—why should anyone make a fuss? Marxists argue that it is not that these figures cannot be lampooned. It is that these *differences* in life-style associated with unequal classes come to be ranked as *better* or *worse*. Of course there is nothing intrinsically superior about modes of dress or food or names or whatever. But there is no doubt whose different attributes come to be ranked as superior and whose as inferior. Why else should people spend thousands of pounds on a public school education for their children if they were not going to be equipped with the 'right', the most 'valuable', social attributes as a result? Public schools are certainly not places where children merely learn academic subjects in a privileged setting. They are self-conscious socialisation agencies, designed to reproduce an elite with elite characteristics. They endow children with the necessary 'cultural capital' to go with their unequal access to material capital. In this way, the ranking of class stereotypes acts as a cultural support to the facts of economic inequality in a capitalist society.

Marxists argue that such an analysis of the relationship between the infrastructure and the superstructure tells us a great deal about *power* in a class society. The dominant class rules but not by necessarily being the actual office-holders who make decisions. It rules because its interests are considered superior by all those—property-owners and property-less alike—who have been subject to socialisation into dominant ideas by superstructural agencies. In Marx's words: *"The ideas of the ruling class are, in every age, the ruling ideas."*

It is for these reasons that the concepts of *false consciousness* and *class consciousness* are of such importance for Marxist theory. Because the subordinate class subscribe to dominant ideologies, which obscure the real nature of class society from their gaze, their picture of the world and their place in it is wrong. Their consciousness of reality, that is, is *false*.

Only when a class-based mode of production falters will members of a subordinate class start to discard their false images of the world and come to see the reality of their exploited status. Then they come to see themselves as they really are—a class. In Marx's words, they develop a *class consciousness*. Their *subjective* view of themselves and their condition comes to match its *objective* reality. It is the emergence of a class consciousness by a subordinate class that is the key which unlocks the revolution which overthrows a mode of production and its dominant class. How does this happen? How does false consciousness becme class consciousness?

As with the existence of false ideas, true consciousness cannot come into being independently of economic circumstances. According to Marx, the impetus for revolution does not arise randomly, or by chance. Ideas about how a society ought to be restructured can only develop under certain circumstances. In particular, when institutional arrangements which have come into being to support a particular mode of production no longer suit its productive relationships, because of changes these have undergone through time, pressure for change builds up. The exploited class then embark on a political struggle designed to replace old social arrangements with ones more suited to new economic arrangements.

Feudalism to Capitalism

In feudal society, the owners of land were the dominant class, owning the dominant means of production. The superstructure supported their dominance, with ideas reflecting their class interests being the ruling ideas. For example, feudal law bound serfs to the land and political power was in the hands of the landlords and nobles. Feudal religion legitimated these arrangements. As one hymn puts it:
"The rich man in his castle,
The poor man at his gate:
God made them high or lowly,
And ordered their estate.,"
For the Marxist there is nothing surprising in this correspondence between the characteristics of production and the character of prevailing ideas. Clearly, if feudal legal, political or religious ideas had stressed something different, feudal production could not have survived. The correspondence between the material world and the world of ideas continues as economic changes take place. As capitalism replaced feudalism, superstructural ideas necessarily changed in consequence, in order to support and justify the *new* economic arrangements, so that *they* could work. According to the Marxist, this is how this happened. As Feudalism progressed, technological innovations began to transform the nature of production, from labour-intensive agriculture to mechanised agriculture, and ultimately to industrial production. As these Agricultural and Industrial Revolutions unfolded, so the new capitalist class emerged as the owners of the foundation of the new and growing means of production—capital.

For a time, however, the superstructure lagged behind these changes, its character still reflecting and legitimating the old economic arrangements. For example, though capitalist production required a mobile labour force and land to be freely available for buying and selling, the old legal and political arrangements prevented this.

Eventually, the strain or contradiction between the interests of the new bourgeoisie and the power and practices of the old land-owning class became too great and the landlord class was overthrown. Though this happened quite quickly and violently in other European societies, the change was begun earlier and was more gradual in Britain. By means of various political alterations, which took place over a few centuries, the landlord class came to share political power, first with the capitalist landowners and then with the new industrialists. Eventually the control of political decision-making passed irrevocably into capitalist hands, though a residue of influence remained with the landlords, even until today.

Capitalism to Communism

Marx predicted that the same kind of process would be apparent in the revolutionary transformation of the capitalist mode of production into the communist one. Again people's ideas and actions would be the motor of this change. However, these revolutionary ideas could only come about as a result of the emergence of class consciousness. This would only happen as capitalism developed as a mode of production. According to Marx, the evolution of capitalism can only occur by means of the progressive exploitation of the working class. That is, though capitalism survives only by exploiting the wage-earning class to a greater and greater extent, an increase in such exploitation will inevitably transform false consciousness into class consciousness. As a result, the steps which are taken to ensure capitalism's 'progress' as a productive system will at the same time guarantee the sowing of the seeds of its own destruction. This is how it is supposed to happen.

As we said earlier, capitalism was established *prior* to the development of industry. But it was only with the *Industrial* Revolution, representing progress for capital, that the reality of capitalist society could start to be visible to its members.

Industrial production created large urban settlements for the first time. Living in the same overcrowded conditions of poverty and squalor and working in the same factory workplaces the urban proletariat could together begin to recognise their common exploited state. Furthermore, as capitalism develops as a mode of production this exploitation increases. As this happens, class consciousness begins to replace false consciousness.

Capitalist production depends upon capital accumulation. Capitalists accumulate capital by increasing the return from the sale of their goods while at the same time lowering the cost of their production. One major way of lowering costs is to cut labour costs by constantly mechanising—decreasing the labour force. This has two effects. First, smaller capitalists, lacking the capital to invest in new machinery are unable to compete successfully. They go to the wall, and join the proletariat-class. Second, unemployment increases among the proletariat. Since wage-earners are also consumers, an increase in the impoverishment of some of them reduces demand for goods. Faced with this loss in demand capitalists have to cut costs still further in order to retain profit levels and remain solvent. This is done by either decreasing their labour forces still further or by reducing wage levels. This can be done in two ways. Wages can be *actually* reduced. (The 1926 General Strike took place when miners' wages were reduced). More topically, they can be 'increased' at a slower rate than the rate of inflation. As a result of either of these methods demand decreases still further and this further affects supply.

As this process continues, the gap in reward between the contracting bourgeoisie and the evergrowing proletariat increases. As the proletariat become increasingly impoverished in this way, so the conditions emerge for the development of a fully-fledged class consciousness among them. The proletariat is thus transformed from being merely an *objective* class—a class in *fact*—to being a *subjective* class—a class in their *thoughts*—as well. As Marx put it, it changes from being just a class *in* itself to being a class *for* itself.

When this class consciousness reaches its fullest extent, the proletariat rise up and overthrow capitalism, taking over the means of production and the state apparatus, as the capitalists had done before them.

According to Marx, this is the final revolution in a society. Unlike earlier revolutions there will be no new exploiting class. Rule by the proletariat means self-government by the workers. Class society is abolished, with all its evils, and a new realm of human freedom begins, in Communist society.

Here, at last, is an abundant society where all benefit, and all are free to live and work in a flexible, creative way *for themselves,* rather than for others. People come to control their own destiny and 'make their own history'. Equality brings emancipation. According to Marx it will be "possible for me to do one thing today and another tomorrow, to hunt in the morning, fish in the afternoon, rear cattle in the evening, criticise after dinner, *just as I have a mind,* without ever becoming hunter, fisherman, shepherd or critic."

So, only in Communist society can human beings fulfil their potential for creativity and goodness. In all other forms of society, the production of material wealth by the dominance of one class over the rest denies this possibility. Despite the ways it is dressed up by those who have power, in the Marxist view all class societies inevitably *alienate* their members, dehumanise them, and deny them the chance of fulfilling their potential. For Marx, in a class society a human being is *prevented* from being truly human.

Functionalist and Marxist theories: a comparison

Like the functionalist, the Marxist argues that social structures come into being independently of people's ideas. (Though ideas are the motor of change for the Marxist, they are determined by economic circumstances occurring prior to the development of these ideas—at the level of the structure of production). Like the functionalist, the Marxist argues that there are prevailing systems of ideas which serve to maintain the social structure. Also like the functionalist, therefore, the Marxist emphasises socialisation into a set of pre-existing beliefs as a key element in the process whereby humans become social beings, and a key factor in enabling the continuity and persistence of social systems. There the similarities end, however.

The functionalist explains the institutional character of a social system in terms of the functions each of the institutions plays in maintaining the system in a state of healthy integration. The process of socialisation is the mechanism whereby individuals arrive at a consensus about how to behave, thus ensuring that the necessary functional roles are acted out properly. The structure of society can be best understood as a *cultural* edifice—a set of normative prescriptions for belief and action. To understand human behaviour, we must look for its *cultural* origins, at the impact of the determinants of the normative world.

For the Marxist, on the other hand, social structures are *material* structures, consisting of groups in possession of unequal economic advantages. Socialisation into the prevailing culture in such class societies is a process whereby inequality is either legitimated for, or obscured from the gaze of, their members—particularly the most disadvantaged. It is, in fact, a major instrument of control, and a primary source of the power of the dominant class. Culture in a class society is a means of propping up an unequal structure without whose support it would collapse.

To understand human behaviour, says the Marxist, we must look at the distribution of economic advantage, of material resources, *not* merely at the determinants of the normative world. Indeed, the status of this realm of social life—a society's culture—is nothing but an *effect,* an outgrowth, of material reality, whose purpose is to legitimate this reality.

So it is not that functionalists *ignore* the existence of material influences on behaviour. Nor is it that Marxists *ignore* the influence of culture. It is a matter of deciding which is cause and which is effect.

For the functionalist, sociological explanation rests on the primacy of culture. For the Marxist it rests on the primacy of economic relationships. For the functionalist the distribution of advantage is an effect of norms and values. For the Marxist, norms and values are effects of the structure of material inequality.

4 Interpretivism

Symbolic Interactionism

Symbolic interactionism is the name given to one of the best-known of interpretive theories. It is with symbolic interactionism that the phrases 'definition of the situation', 'reality is in the eye of the beholder' and, 'If men define situations as real, they are real in their consequences' are most usually associated.

Though rather cumbersome, the name given to this perspective does clearly indicate the kinds of human activity which its proponents consider it essential to concentrate on in order to understand how social life is possible. According to SI theorists, social life literally is the 'interaction of humans by the use of symbols'. That is, they are interested

1. in the way in which humans employ symbols of what they mean in order to communicate with one another (an orthodox interpretive interest)
2. in the effects that the interpretation of these symbols have on the behaviour of the parties to an occasion of social interaction.

In our earlier discussion of interpretivism, we emphasised how the behaviour of human beings must essentially be the product of how they interpret the world around them. It is not behaviour which is *learnt* or *determined,* as structural theories suggest. Rather, it is *chosen* as appropriate behaviour in the light of how people *define* the situations they encounter—what they take social settings to *mean*.

But a question we did not consider earlier is this. How far does this process of interpretation which, according to the interpretivist, is always the origin of behaviour, affect the *other* people involved in these meaningful encounters? This is clearly important. As we said in Chapter 1, most of the situations in which we find ourselves during the course of our journey through life are inevitably *social* situations—they involve *other* people doing things. Nearly every time we interpret meaning in order to decide how to act we are interpreting the actions of other human beings.

One of the principal interests of SI has been to consider this very question—the effects of interpretation *on the person whose actions are being interpreted.*

SI stresses that *interaction* is a two-way interpretive process. We must not only understand that someone's action is a product of how *they* have interpreted the behaviour of someone else, but that this interpretation will have an impact on the action whose behaviour has been interpreted in certain ways too. One of the major contributions of symbolic interactionism to interpretive theory has been to elaborate and explain the different kinds of effects which the interpretations of others can have on the social identities of the individuals who are the objects of these interpretations.

The construction of self-image

The most common effect is that we use the interpretations of others—what they take our behaviour to mean—as evidence of who *we* think we are. That is, our *self*-image is a product of the way others think of us.

For SI this is largely what socialisation means. It is not, as structural theorists argue, a process whereby given external, cultural rules are generally internalised by people. It is an outcome of the interpretive process—the allocation of meaning between people—that for interpretivists, is at the root of all social interaction. Our personalities are constructed by means of this interpreting process as follows.

During the course of our lives, we encounter a particular number of people, all of whom take our behaviour towards them to symbolise something about our *selves*. They interpret our behaviour in the light of the evidence they are provided with. They then act towards us in the light of this interpretation, indicating via the symbolic means available to them what kind of person they have decided we are. The image we have of ourselves is crucially influenced by these *re*actions to us of the particular individuals we come into contact with. We cannot ignore what kind of person others are telling us we are; the image of our 'self' is seriously affected by the image others have of us.

Take, for example, the relationship between a primary school teacher and his/her class. Being human, the teacher cannot help but make judgements about the children in the class, particularly about their ability. Equally, according to SI, since the children are human too, their view of themselves and their abilities cannot help but be influenced by the judgements of the teacher. So the little boy who sits attentively in the front of the class, behaves well and politely and is keen and conscientious, is likely to be thought of as 'intelligent' or 'able'. In contrast, the girl who sits at the back of the class persistently misbehaving and is inattentive and lazy, is less favourably interpreted.

SI argues that often what matters is not whether the interpretations are correct but the impact they can have on their recipients. In this case, even though the children are in fact of the same ability, the teacher has decided they are not, and as a result treats them differently. The little boy is encouraged to work whereas the little girl is merely admonished for mis-behaviour and kept under control.

These different reactions of the teacher influence the way the children see themselves. Sustained by the support and encouragement of the teacher the little boy works hard and fulfills his potential. Persuaded by the teacher's reactions that she has little academic ability, the little girl concentrates merely on larking about. The teacher's judgements are thus confirmed; the prophesy about the children's abilities comes true. The justice of the interpretations matters less than the consequence of their application, particularly for the way their recipients are encouraged to see themselves.

The fortuity of the outcome of this process of interaction between interpreter and interpreted is plain to see. Our 'self'—the person we become—depends upon the *particular* people we happen to encounter in our journey through life. *Other* parents, friends, acquaintances, workmates, etc., could have made us into very different people. In our example, a different teacher might have encouraged both children equally, with much more positive consequences for the little girl's self-image.

But the influence of the interpretations of others is only one half of the process of interaction emphasised by SI. Far from human personality being simply the passive construction of others, SI stresses the *active* role which humans play in the creation of their social selves. According to SI since we soon come to learn that others will interpret our behaviour our *own* interpretive abilities allow us to manipulate these interpretations to suit our vision of ourselves. We use our capacity to be *self-reflexive* in order to present the person we wish others to think we are. We play roles in a *creative* way to elicit from others the responses we desire. In effect, we manage, or orchestrate, the responses of others by presenting the image of our self we wish them to hold. We become actors on the stage of life, writing our own lines. We 'create' our selves by organising the reactions of others in our encounters with them.

The SI theorist most commonly associated with this emphasis on creative role-playing is Erving Goffman. In a book called *The Presentation of Self in Everyday Life,* Goffman outlines his conception of social life as a stage upon which humans play themselves, and explains the social props the dramatis personae press into service to present these selves to others.

Interpretivism

According to Goffman, very few human attributes, possessions or activities are not used in this theatrical way. The clothes we wear, where we live, the house we live in, they way we furnish it, the ways we walk and talk, the work we do and the ways in which we spend our leisure time etc. etc.—indeed everything that is public about ourselves can, and is, used to tell others what kind of person we are. We thus 'manage' the information we provide for others. We control the impact our dress, appearance and habits will have in order that others will be encouraged to see us as the people we are claiming to be.

For Goffman and his fellow interactionists then, socialisation is essentially about the triumph of the creative capacities of the individual over the reactions of others. Not all interpretivists agree however. *Labelling theory* is a perspective which has grown out of symbolic interactionism. Though it has a great deal in common with SI's main emphases, labelling theory is less interested in the ways in which people *are* able to influence others' interpretations of themselves than in the kinds of interaction where no such opportunities exist. Labelling theorists are mainly interested in the fact that sometimes people are victims, often helpless, of the interpretations, or *labels,* of others to such an extent that their social identities *can* be imposed upon them, even against their will.

Why should this happen? Why should we find ourselves in social situations where we *cannot* manipulate the interpretations of others?

Labelling Theory: the person as victim

1 Labels which contradict self-image

Sometimes we are in no position to protest against misinterpretation because we are dead. For example, as we have already briefly discussed in Chapter 1, a verdict of suicide depends on the interpretations of a range of people—kin, friends, policemen and, in particular, coroners. Though bodies communicate as loudly as they can to tell us the truth, everything eventually depends on others' interpretations. As we shall see later, (Chapter 5), those charged with deciding the cause of someone's death can sometimes pay little heed to the efforts of suicides to manipulate the label they desired.

A rather more gruesome possibility is of someone being labelled as dead who is actually alive but in no position to alter the label. In such a case, the diagnosis of death becomes the ultimate self-fulfilling prophecy. After all, the victim of any such mis-interpretation is clearly powerless to halt his/her burial or cremation or else the diagnosis wouldn't have been made in the first place. Of course, if a mistake *is* made in this area of social definition it is less likely to be discovered than in any other.

Yet the possibility of a wrong diagnosis is always there. On the extremely few occasions where we have evidence from exhumation (undertaken for reasons other than doubt concerning whether or not the body was dead before burial, of course) the incidence of bodies having moved, or being found in postures of distress and mental torment must lead us to suspect that even in this final act of the interpretation of others, humans are as fallible as in any other social setting. Confirmation of this suspicion is difficult to come by, of course, but a little is available from the few people who have lived to tell the tale of being wrongly labelled as dead.

Sometimes we *can* protest against a wrong label but this cuts no ice with our interpreters. For example it is the public labelling of a shoplifter in Court and later on in the local press, that will be the evidence others will go on, not our protestations of innocence.

In any case, sometimes our protestations are merely seen as confirmation of the appropriateness of the label. For example, if you are diagnosed as being mentally ill even though you consider yourself perfectly sane, it is likely that you will make a considerable fuss about the prospect of being carted off to a mental hospital. Normal though this reaction may be from your point of view, the danger is that your angry or excitable behaviour will be seen by others that they were right to label you as unbalanced. 'After all, no *normal* person would get in that state'.

The consequences of the application of the label of 'dead' to somebody provides another example. In countries where bodies are routinely embalmed, the agents used in this process (eg formaldehyde) often give rise to physical reactions which are akin to life. For example, the body can move, and, apparently, respire. Of course, where embalming is taking place, such symptoms will be interpreted as *its* result, rather than evidence of life. So, in such circumstances, if a living person wrongly diagnosed and being embalmed is nevertheless able to produce some bodily movement this will simply serve to confirm the label. As a result, the prophesy soon *will* become fulfilled, of course.

Finally, even if we rise above the interpretations of others and attempt to *ignore* what we consider a wrong label and act normally, it is perfectly possible that this too can simply serve to confirm its justice for others. For example, when you are diagnosed as mentally ill, if you *don't* make a fuss and act as normally as possible in order to prove your sanity, this too may simply be interpreted as confirmation of your diagnosed condition. 'After all, no *normal* person would just *sit* there like that'.

Goffman's classic interactionist account of hoarding behaviour among mental patients (*Asylums* 1968) is a very good example of the confirmatory character of 'normal' behaviour once the label of 'abnormal' has been securely enough applied.

Hoarding behaviour is a very common feature of the behaviour of patients in mental hospitals. All sorts of apparently useless and trivial objects—like pieces of string, toilet paper etc.—are constantly in the possession of many of the inmates who steadfastly refuse to let them out of their sight for a moment. The usual interpretation of this behaviour serves to confirm the label attached to the patient. It is argued that it is obviously abnormal to have such worthless items permanently about one's person and such hoarding can only be a reflection of considerable and deep-seated anxieties and insecurities.

Goffman disputes this analysis, arguing that it only seems appropriate from the standpoint of life *out*side the mental hospital, where such 'useless' items are always available. Inside the institution, however, where, for the inmate, they are much more difficult to come by, it makes very good sense to look after them very carefully. Furthermore, since mental hospital patients tend to lack both privacy and storage facilities the obvious place to keep them secure is about their persons.

All of these examples, then, are of victims of mis-interpretations whose contradictory accounts either can't be heard or won't be listened to.

Labelling theory argues that sometimes the process of labelling can be so overwhelming that even the victims of mis-interpretation cannot resist its impact. Faced with a label completely contradicting their view of themselves being consistently and persistently applied by others, the original self-images of the labelled persons crumble under the onslaught. They come to see themselves anew, embracing the alternative images others have applied to them.

As in the earlier effects of labelling, the correctness or 'truth' of the label has little to do with the power of its impact. Right or wrong in *fact*, its application and the reactions of others to its existence *make* it true. Once again, the prophecy is fulfilled, but in this case it becomes the reality for both the beholder *and* the beheld.

2 The alteration of self-image

The identification of this process has been a feature of the application of labelling theory to deviance—the area where it has probably been most influential. One of its most significant contributions to the study of deviant behaviour has been not only to show that the identification of deviance is a product of the interpretation of a particular individual in a particular social setting (as is all labelling). It has also shown that the reactions of others to a labelled deviant are often so severe that they produce a dramatic alteration in an already established self-image.

Lemert and Paranoia

Edwin Lemert's famous account of the social construction of paranoia demonstrates both these aspects of labelling very clearly. Paranoia is a mental condition in which the sufferer imagines he or she is being persecuted by a well-organised conspiracy. However, as Lemert points out, if paranoia is suspected in somebody then such a conspiracy actually does come into being. The 'ill' person is observed secretly. Since mentally disturbed people don't know what's good for them and can act irrationally, attempts to organise treatment will also be clandestine: visits to doctors and psychiatric hospitals will be organised behind the patient's back. Any suspicion on the part of the suspected paranoid that this sort of thing is going on will, naturally enough, lead him or her to complain about it. Normal though such resentment may be from the labelled person's standpoint, in the eyes of its applicators this will merely serve to confirm the justice of the label. Clearly, here *is* someone who believes he or she is being conspired against by others. The fact that this is actually what *is* happening won't deter the labellers from having their judgement confirmed!

Such confirmation may lead to a stay in a mental hospital for treatment. It is at this stage in the construction of paranoia that persons so labelled experience the most sustained pressure on their self-images. However certain of their sanity prior to institutionalisation, Lemert argues that the organisational confirmation of the label, particularly by means of deliberate attempts to change behaviour, finally sinks the inmates' previously-held self-images without trace. The suspicion grows that maybe everyone else had it right all along and they were too ill to appreciate their condition. After all, why else would they be in hospital?

For the labellers of such people, particularly the psychiatric staff, this stage of self-image alteration—an acknowledgement of the need for treatment—is the first major step en route to cure. The fact that it might simply be the *last* stage in the *social* construction of a mental condition which began not with any real illness but with an initial labelling by others, is, of course, not considered.

The impact which *organisational* labelling is designed to have on the construction of social personality, and, particularly, on the creation of a new self-image, has also been powerfully articulated by Goffman.

Goffman and Institutionalisation

According to Goffman, the official treatment of many kinds of deviant behaviour in organisations set up for the purpose, is, as in the case of mental illness, a quite self-conscious attempt to alter the deviant's self-image, so that he or she may become more amenable to 'cure'. In a celebrated account of what he calls 'total institutions' Goffman advances the view that establishments like prisons, concentration camps and mental hospitals, where labelled deviants are completely incarcerated over considerable periods, are essentially agencies of re-socialisation. Though his argument is not confined to the treatment of deviants (he claims the same principles underpin the rigorous training undergone by, for example, soldiers and the members of some religious orders) the *involuntary* nature of the deviants' membership of such institutions makes any successful alteration to *their* self-images particularly noteworthy.

Goffman defines total institutions as 'places of residence and work where a large number of like-situated individuals cut off from the wider society for an appreciable period of time, together lead an enforced, formally administered round of life'. He argues that in such establishments, the organisation of life is deliberately designed to strip the inmate of his or her self-image and replace it with one more acceptable to the ethos of the institution. He calls this process 'institutionalisation'.

For example, he says, admission procedures are often designed to remove all visible symbols of the inmate's former self and replace them with indications of the new person he or she is to be trained to be. Thus, names are often replaced by numbers, as in prisons, concentration camps and military establishments, or by new names, as in religious orders. The inmate's physical appearance is sometimes altered as visibly as possible: clothing is often removed on entry and replaced with institutional uniforms and hair is cut in a severe fashion. Since the acquisition of possessions may be frowned upon and made difficult (cf. our earlier reference to the hoarding behaviour characteristic of mental patients) all or most personal property is often confiscated on entry. Personal space may be denied, even for the most private of activities.

In these kinds of ways, and others, says Goffman, the aim is to strip the inmates of the props by which they retained a sense of their former selves and were able to communicate this to others.

Furthermore, these attempts to alter the self of the inmate can be reinforced by its *debasement,* in ritual and other ways—a process Goffman calls the *'mortification of the self'.* For example, new inmates may have to undergo humiliation upon entry, such as strip-searching (in prison) or ritual ablution (in mental hospital). During their incarceration inmates are often obliged to behave in the most obsequious and obedient manner to the institution's staff, sometimes in the face of provocation. Such degradations, often in public, are designed, argues Goffman, to mortify the former self of the inmate, to render it soiled and thereafter unusable, and encourage its replacement by a new identity, more suitable to meet the demands of the institution.

Though labelling theorists would normally expect such processes to prove irresistible to their recipients, Goffman is true to his interactionist principles. Believing that social identities are not just imposed on people but are created and re-created as a two-way interpretive process, Goffman stresses not only the impact of institutionalisation but the capacity of inmates to resist or adjust to the processes to which they are subjected to a greater or lesser degree. He thus not only talks of those who do become 'colonised', or institutionalised, preferring life in the institution to life outside, or who become 'converted', acquiescing to the staff's view of the model inmate and acting out the role to the limit. He also talks of inmates who protect their selves by withdrawing from interaction with others, or who do so by actively rebelling against the institution, as well as of those (the majority, in Goffman's view) who do so by 'playing it cool'—who stay out of trouble and maintain their self-image by playing whatever reactive role circumstances demand.

Labelling relations as power relations

If some labelling involves *victimisation* of the kind we have been discussing then labelling theory argues that we have to ask a further, final question: Where do these victims come from? For example, why do some people come to be labelled as mentally ill and not others? Why do *certain* children come to be labelled as uneducable and not others?

For labelling theorists the answer lies not in any reality of different mental conditions or levels of intelligence. Rather, it lies in the origin of the *perception* of these attributes by others. The focus is on the reasons for these kinds of labels being attached to *certain kinds of people* rather than any characteristics the victims of these labels may or may not possess. The interesting question is therefore not 'How did these people *get* like this?' but 'Why did *these* people come to be labelled like this and not others?' or 'Why are *these* people the victims of such labels and not other people?'

The usual labelling theory answer to these questions is that the application of such labels is ultimately about the exercise of *power*. According to labelling theory the most damaging labels in social life—those of *deviant*—usually become attached to the most helpless and least powerful members of society—those least capable of fighting back and resisting the process. This analysis of deviant labelling as a reflection of the exercise of power is described by Howard Becker, one of its leading exponents, as the process whereby the *'underdogs'* in a society become the victims of its *'overdogs'*.

This is a feature of labelling approaches to deviant behaviour in general: deviants are generally seen as the victims, not as the wrongdoers. It is particularly evident in the typical labelling analysis of *crime*. An examination of this approach not only makes it plain that here crime is seen exclusively as a product of labelling and of the all-pervading impact the allocation of such a label can have. It also shows how labelling theory sees the relations between labellers and labelled in this kind of area of social life as essentially power relations. Quite contrary to the conventional view then, the victims are the underdogs who are made into criminals whereas the wrongdoers are the more powerful overdogs who impel the powerless down a never-ending spiral of criminal deviance.

Labelling theorists argue that there are two fundamental questions which have to be asked about crime.

1 Since there cannot be crime without laws, why do *some* human activities come to be made illegal and not others?
2 Since there cannot be criminals unless people break laws *and* are caught, why do *some* people become criminals and not others?

According to labelling theory, the answers to both these questions reflect the distribution of power in society. Not only are the powerful able to designate those acts which are illegal in a society but they are also able to influence who gets labelled as a criminal.

Laws

Labelling theory argues that though we might like to think that laws are somehow God-given or quite definitely in *everyone's* best interest, things are not quite as cosy as this. They stress that we have to recognise that the construction of legal rules is a *political* act. The decision that *this* act should be allowed whereas another should not is a decision made by humans who have the power to do so. Furthermore, 'the powerful' in this regard doesn't simply mean the *actual* law-makers. It also includes those individuals or groups who are able to *influence* the decisions of the law-makers—those people in a society whom Becker calls its 'moral entrepreneurs'.

Because of this relationship between power and the construction of legal rules, it is not surprising, say labelling theorists, that the acts that are not illegal in a society tend to be the acts in which the powerful engage. So, although it is perfectly possible to imagine a society in which it is *illegal* to inherit wealth, or profit from rent, or exploit black labour in South African mines, or avoid paying taxes, yet *legal* to smoke marijuhana, make homosexual advances in public, and engage in 'adult' activity at a much younger age than 18, this is not how things are. Laws reflect the distribution of power in that the less powerful are more likely to engage in those activities which the laws prohibit.

You might consider this a rather far-fetched view. After all, what about laws prohibiting tax evasion or the placement of contracts by public officials in return for reward, or company fraud or the monopolisation of production etc? Labelling theory grants that of course there are *some* laws which particularly affect the activities of say, the wealthy, but argues that these *tend to be the laws whch are least strenuously enforced*. And even if they are vigorously enforced they tend to be the laws least likely to furnish a successful prosecution, because of the resouces available to the powerful to defend themselves.

In effect then, the SI position is that the role of power in the construction of crime is not just restricted to the *definition* of illegal acts but influences the *investigation* of crime too. And nowhere is this latter influence more apparent than in the selection of the individual criminal to prosecute—the labelling of a particular person's actions as illegal.

Law-breaking

Why should some people be labelled as criminals and not others? The obvious answer to this is that only some people choose to commit crime. From this point of view, the job of any explanation of criminality—sociological, psychological or biological—is to discover what it is about these kinds of people that led them down the criminal path.

For labelling theory, however, things are not as straightforward as this, primarily because such an analysis ignores the huge discrepancy between the number of crimes committed and the number of criminals convicted.

Research demonstrates without doubt that the incidence of criminal activity bears little relation to the number of crimes known to the police (the C.K.P. index) and even less to the number of crimes for which the police get a conviction (the 'clear-up' rate).

The most recent piece of research into crime, the British Crime Survey (March 1983) demonstrates this as clearly as previous research had done. 11,000 households were interviewed in order to identify the crimes they had suffered and the results compared with the C.K.P. index. The survey shows that 5 times as many violent crimes and 4 times as many property crimes are committed as are reported to the police. The degree to which the official statistics underplay the real level of crime depends on the particular category of crime. Almost all cars which are stolen are reported. It is the only way owners can receive compensation from the insurance companies. Probably for the same reason (because more private property is now insured than before) the number of burglaries reported has increased; the survey suggests one out of 2 are now reported. But other property crimes have much lower reporting rates. e.g. only 13% of acts of vandalism were reported and it is estimated that probably only 1% of all shoplifting offences are reported. Why should crimes be so underreported?

Many crimes, e.g. vandalism, are not reported because of their petty nature. Yet even many violent crimes go unreported. e.g. only about 20% of all woundings, sexual attacks and robberies are reported. The main reason for this low rate seems to be the young age of many of the victims and their lack of faith in either the way the police will handle the complaint or the capacity of the police to solve the crime.

Earlier studies have shown that even when crimes get reported to the police they do not always get recorded. Among the reasons for this include overwork, doubts about the validity of the allegations and a temptation to improve the clear-up rates by not including unsolvable crimes.

As well as such *victim surveys, self-report studies* also illustrate the wide gap between the commission of crime and the C.K.P. index and the even wider gap between commission and clear-up. Such studies ask people to volunteer their past illegal actions under a guarantee of absolute confidentiality. They reveal that anything between 50% and 90% of people admit some kind of illegal behaviour which could result in a court appearance if detected. Even more significant, they also indicate that criminal activity is distributed across all sections of society. They show that crimes are just as likely to be committed by the middle-class as by the working-class and certainly demonstrate the error of assuming that crime is more likely to be concentrated in the lower strata of the class structure.

Yet this is precisely what the official conviction statistics—of crimes cleared up by the police—*do* indicate. The overwhelming impression from these figures is that crime is mainly committed by the young, male, urban working-class.

Why should this be? If, as self-report studies indicate, crime is *committed* by no *particular kind* of person, why do only certain kinds of people get *caught*?

The labelling theory answer, of course, is that only certain kinds of people are likely to be *labelled* as criminal. Being human, police can only take action against acts and people they *perceive* as breaking the law. *That* is why certain kinds of people become criminals. It is not because they are the only people who have committed crimes. Indeed it is not even because they necessarily *have* committed any crime at all. It is simply because they have been *interpreted* as having done so.

Why is there such a distinctive pattern to these interpretations? Labelling theorists argue that the perceptions of the police inevitably emanate from the stereotypes of criminals with which they and other agents of law enforcement operate.

Why stereotypes should prevail in law enforcement is clear enough. If, as self-report studies show, criminal activity is distributed equally throughout any population, then whatever stereotype of the 'typical criminal' you choose to operate, your judgement is going to be vindicated. But the important question is: Why have *some* stereotypes come to prevail in the pursuit of crime and not others?

According to labelling theory, we need look no further for our answer than at the distribution of power in society. In the same way that the powerful are able to influence the designation of certain *acts* as illegal rather than others, so they are able to encourage certain *perceptions of the criminal*—advantageous to themselves—to prevail. So, although the official conviction statistics tell us very little about the actual distribution of crime in society, they do tell us much about the kinds of people policemen and other law enforcers are most likely to label as criminal and, in turn, about the kinds of influences on such stereotypes employed in law enforcement the powerful have been able to bring to bear. The picture painted by the conviction statistics makes this clear. The chances of you matching up to the stereotypes typically employed in law enforcement decreases as you move up the social hierarchy. Criminal labels await the least advantaged members of society because they are powerless: "... we should not be surprised to find blacks and working-class people over-represented in the official statistics of crime, since they and their behaviour are more likely to fit law-enforcement agencies' perceptions of 'criminals' and 'crime', and they are less likely to be able to mobilise the material and social resources necessary to convince others that 'they're not like that'." (Bilton et al).

Of course, once the powerless receive their labels, the self-fulfilling prophecy we've just referred to will come into effect. The successful application of the stereotype will mean its validity is confirmed for its users and it can be employed with even *more* conviction in the future. The process of criminal labelling thus *in*creases the chances of the least powerful becoming criminals and *de*creases the chances of the most powerful. In this way, inequalities of power in society are cemented by the process of law enforcement. Furthermore, once the stereotype is applied and the label is attached, the existence of the label promotes the usual self fulfilling prophecy so far as any particular individual actor is concerned. Others react to the label in such a way that makes future 'normal' activity very difficult. Because of a conviction, other people may ostracise or treat with suspicion the labelled person, occupational opportunities may become unavailable and so on. The *'stigma'* of being branded a criminal overwhelms all other attributes; something someone is supposed to have *done* becomes what he or she *is*. Because of the reactions of others to the stigma of the label, the labelled person—whether guilty or innocent in *fact*—is, according to labelling theory, often impelled into pursuing the 'career' of a criminal, simply because all other normal options are closed down.

Obviously, this process of being forced into a deviant career by the reactions of others—known as *deviance amplification*—is not as immediately problematic for the self as, say, the misinterpretation of mental illness. After all, one usually knows whether one *was* guilty of an offence or not. Nevertheless, it can still mean the labelled person's self-image is in danger of alteration, especially if the opportunities for a 'normal' existence are sufficiently restricted. Lacking any choice, labelled persons come to see themselves as the person they have been forced to become.

In an area such as crime, therefore, structuralist and interpretive assumptions meet head on. Pursuing the external determinants of any social activity located in the social structure, the structural theorist looks for the reasons why, as the conviction statistics show, certain kinds of people come to commit criminal acts and some not. Armed with the conviction statistics which feature the urban working-class male above all other categories of person, structuralist explanations of crime attempt to identify the reasons why a person in this sort of structural location is impelled to commit crime more often than other kinds of person.

One of the most popular explanations of this phenomenon is known as *sub-cultural theory*. Here crime is explained as the product of cultural or normative influences. The young working-class male more often than any other kind of person finds himself in a cultural setting where crinimal activity is normal and where conformity to such norms via socialisation gives rise to law-breaking. The sociological task is therefore to identify those cultural features that promote crime in this kind of social world and not in others.

As in the case of all structuralist explanations, then, the emphasis is on identifying the origins of the *external* social forces whose existence is manifested in the behaviour of individuals.

In contrast, labelling theory's approach to crime feature the opposed interpetive assumptions about social behaviour. Armed with *their* evidence—that crime is much more widespread among all social groups than the *conviction* rates show—labelling theory is interested not in why young working-class males *commit* crimes more often than other people but why they are more likely to be *labelled* as criminals more often than others. The interesting questions here therefore concern the reasons for *their* behaviour being interpreted as criminal while other peoples' is not. The labelling perspective thus focusses on the social construction of the reality of crime by the members of a society themselves rather than on the determining influence on their behaviour of a structural reality outside of these members.

Yet, as the study of crime also shows, the structuralist and SI emphases are not as mutually exclusive as they might at first appear. The reason is that SI does not embrace a completely interpretive approach to social life. We can see this in two aspects of its explanation of crime.

First, the idea of 'stereotypes' in the application of criminal labels refers to generally-held views among those whose job it is to enforce the law. Since such generally-held views will, for example, be encountered and embraced and therefore perpetuated by new recruits to the Force, this is clearly much closer to the structuralist view of socialisation into pre-existing normative definitions than pure interpretivism allows.

Second, the idea that powerful groups influence both the construction

Interpretivism

of laws and the stereotypes of the criminal which directs law enforcement is quite close to an orthodox structuralist perspective. For such a process to take place, particular groups have to have the power to exercise influence and others to lack the resources to resist. This vision of social life as being crucially influenced by the unequal distribution of advantage between groups is, of course, a conventional structural-conflict standpoint.

The reason for this apparent contradiction is that sociological theories, especially when put into practice to explain a particular area of social life, are usually neither completely structural nor completely interpretive. SI is a fairly moderate version of interpretivism, which, while emphasising the primacy of interpretation in the social construction of reality, doesn't deny the existence of a fund of commonly-held definitions—a common culture, if you like—from which people choose their interpretations. Furthermore, the fact that it insists upon a recognition of the existence of some kind of structure of power and advantage within which the labelling of deviants takes place also shows that it cannot be seen as adopting a fully-fledged *anti*-structuralist position.

In this sense, SI occupies the middle ground between pure structuralism and pure interpretivism. In fact, as you will discover, most sociological theories are found somewhere between these extremes, not concentrating exclusively on either external determinants or interpretation but emphasising one rather than the other. Most definitely at the interpretive extreme, however, is ethnomethodology.

Ethnomethodology

Ethnomethodology pushes the interpretive case—that social reality is the creation of actors—to the limit. To put it very crudely, it rests upon three assumptions.
1   Social life is inherently precarious. Anything could happen in social interaction. However
2   actors never realise this, because
3   they unwittingly possess the practical abilities necessary to make the world appear an ordered place.

The primary ethnomethodological interest is rather different from that of other interpretivists. Instead of being concerned mainly with the *outcome* of interpretation—the creation of self-image, or the consequences of labelling, for example—it focuses on *how* interpretation is arrived at. Ethnomethodology literally means 'people's methods'. The aim is to reveal the methods used by the participants ('members') in any particular social occasion to communicate to each other what they think is going on—what the occasion means to them—and the efforts they each make to have this interpretation corroborated by the others. Ethnomethodology is not interested in 'the' social world but on specific pieces of interaction between members. The stress is on how the order in a social occasion is the accomplishment of its particpants.

This interest in describing these practical abilities of members derives from a theory of social life called *phenomenology*. Phenomenology emphasises that things and events have no meaning in themselves. They only mean that which human beings take them to mean. It stresses that for the members of such a meaningfully created world to live together they must share meanings. They must agree about what things are. Social order depends upon such shared meanings.

Members *do* share meanings. This is because of the way they interpret reality. They do so by using 'commonsense knowledge'. This is embodied in the language we learn. Through language we acquire an enormous amount of knowledge about the world, knowledge we can take for granted others who speak our language possess too. Only a tiny number of things we know about have we actually experienced. The rest of the knowledge, shared with other members, is sense that is common to us all. As the founder of phenomenology in sociology, Alfred Schutz, puts it: "If we put a letter in the mailbox we assume that anonymous fellow-men, called postmen, will perform a series of manipulations, unknown and unobservable to us, with the effect that the addressee, possibly also unknown to us, will receive the message and react in a way which also escapes our sensory observation; and the result of this is that we receive the book we have ordered." (Schutz). Because members can take for granted this shared knowledge about reality they can also take for granted the reality it describes. They can assume the world is a given, objective place. It must be. After all, we *all know* what it is and what happens in it.

This concept of shared, commonsense, knowledge may sound rather like the consensus theorist's notion of culture. But culture refers to a body of rules whose *obedience* by actors explains social order. For the ethnomethodologist commonsense knowledge is *used* by members to *create* order on a particular occasion which would otherwise lack it. Ethnomethodologists define their task as showing how members do this.

Armed with commonsense knowledge and with a confident belief in the factual, ordered, character of the world, members can go ahead and

Interpretivism

make sense of any occasion in which they participate. Ethnomethodology stresses that each social occasion is unique. The words people utter, the actions they take, only have any sense in the particular occasion in which they are used. But they also stress that members, unwittingly engaged in identifying order and an objective reality, see things differently. They identify the similarities of an event with other events. They select from all the things happening around them evidence which supports the view that things which exist or which happen are *typical* of the world. For them an occasion is 'a lecture', 'a dance' or 'a meeting'. In this way a pattern is imposed by the application of commonsense knowledge. By commonsense knowledge too, the gaps in the accounts of happenings by others are filled in by members to reassure themselves that things are as they seem.

This is how R.J. Anderson describes a famous analysis of a two-year old child's story by Harvey Sacks:
"The baby cried.
The mummy picked it up."
Sacks makes the following observations about the story:

a He hears the mummy as the mummy of the baby.
b Any other hearer will, on a first hearing, hear that too. This hearing can always be revised, but it is the *first* hearing.
c There is a relationship between the actions described. The mummy picked up the baby because it was crying.
d We can all make these findings without specific knowledge of the mummy or the baby in question nor of the child who told the story.

The import of this last observation is enormous, for if it is the case that competent users of the English language are able to find the same things from the same fragment of talk, then the methods that are used to do so must be of the highest order of generality. They must be part of the foundations of our common culture." (Anderson, in Meighan, Shelton and Marks).

Without realising it, members thus create the meanings events have. They work at making them mean something. Having arrived at an interpretation, they then have this confirmed by the corroboration of the other participants. The founder of ethnomethodology, Harold Garfinkel, delighted in showing how this could be done even when the corroboration is actually lacking. This is how Paul Filmer describes a very well known Garfinkel experiment designed to demonstrate the lengths members will go to create meaning, to discover the sense in an occasion, in spite of deliberate efforts to frustrate them. "Ten undergraduates were asked to participate in research being carried out by a university's department of psychiatry to explore alternative means of psychotherapy. Each was asked to discuss the background to a serious problem on which he wanted advice, and then to address to an experimenter—who had been falsely presented to him as a trainee student counsellor—a number of questions about it which would be amenable to monosyllabic 'Yes' or 'No' answers. The subject and the experimenter/counsellor were physically separated, and communicated by two-way radio. After the answer to each of his questions had been given, the subject was asked to tape-record his comments upon it, out of radio-hearing of the experimenter/counsellor. The subjects were told that it was usual to ask ten questions, and they were, of course, led to believe that they would be given bona fide answers to them. The experimenter/counsellors, however, were given a list of monosyllabic answers, evenly divided between "yes" and "no", but whose order had been predecided from a table of random numbers. Thus, in this experiment, certain crucial variables of everyday interaction situations had been neutralized: the shared language of subject and experimenter had been reduced to the verbal spoken dimension (intonation, in all probability, would also have been relatively unimportant as an agent of meaning, owing to the distortion of spoken sounds by radio); there was no chance of gestures or physical expressions intervening in the communication process because of the physical separation of subject and experimenter. Also, the possibility of the experimenter/counsellor's answers making sense to the subjects depended entirely on their interpretations of them; indeed, the possibility of answers even being those anticipated by the subjects was reduced to a matter of chance. Garfinkel publishes two unedited transcripts of the exchanges and of the subjects' comments upon them (see Garfinkel (1967), plus a detailed explication of his interpretive findings from them. The burden of these is where the random answers to the carefully thought out and phrased questions of the subjects appeared nonsensical, irrational or in some other way inappropriate or unexpected, then the subject reinterpreted them by reformulating what he assumed to be the context of meaning he held in common with the experimenter/counsellor (and which he had attempted to communicate to the experimenter/counsellor by the phrasing and content of his questions), in order that the latter's responses made sense after all. Even where a succession of plainly contradictory answers engendered the suspicion in the subject that he was being tricked, he appeared reluctant to proceed upon the assumption that this was so." (Filmer, in Filmer et al).

Here, then, is a very different kind of sociology from the others we have been looking at. For structural theorists the most significant features of human social life are forces external to the individual actor.

Interpretivism

To understand social behaviour we have to understand the structural determinants of people's lives. For interactionists/labelling theorists, the actor comes to the fore. Whether being in control of the interpretations of others or being a more passive recipient of their labels, the focus is on the capacities of human beings for meaningful interaction. To understand social action we must understand the processes of interpretation that give rise to it.

For ethnomethodologists, however, the interest is different. They criticise other sociological approaches for taking for granted what they believe is actually the essence of social life. Ethnomethodology is concerned to describe the methods members use to arrive at their own understanding of social occasions, though not the understanding itself. It is interested in the practice of making sense of the world, in how members accomplish social life. Though members are the architects of social order, ethnomethodology wants to know not *what* they build, but *how* they build it.

5 Theory and Method in Sociology

One of the central issues in sociology concerns how the sociologist should go about collecting knowledge of social life. Since you have to decide what your subject-matter is before you can decide how to investigate it, clearly, issues of research methods in sociology cannot be separated from theoretical debates.

Very crudely, we can state the relationship between theory and method in sociology like this (much as we did at the end of chapter one). Structural theorists, who believe social behaviour to be the product of external social forces, are most likely to argue for the use of scientific methods to acquire knowledge of these structural forces. Though much conflict theory uses science to a degree to reveal unequal social structures, the mission to create a fully-fledged science of society is more closely associated with consensus theory.

Interpretive theorists, in contrast, see things rather differently. For them, social behaviour is the outcome of people's abilities to interpret the world around them. Consequently, they believe that science is a wholly inappropriate way of acquiring understanding of social life.

Though not everyone defines science this way, the name given to the set of principles and procedures which is usually accepted to underpin scientific activity is positivism. We will look briefly at a simple version of these principles and procedures now and then analyse why structuralists, and particularly consensus theorists, look upon them with such favour and interpretivists with such disfavour.

Positivism

The guiding principle for the scientist is that if something exists in nature it has been caused by something else in nature. That is, natural phenomena cause other natural phenomena. For example, when water reaches a certain temperature (cause) it freezes (effect). Furthermore, this always happens. There are no circumstances (depending on atmospheric pressure) when water will not become ice at a particular temperature. Such invariable cause and effect relationships are called

Laws. Science sets out to discover the laws of nature. These laws are 'given' for us. Whether we like it or not, water *will* freeze at a certain temperature. Whether we like it or not, the temperature *is* higher in the summer than in the winter. Whether we like it or not, leaves *will* fall from deciduous trees in the autumn. We live in a natural world that is organised in a particular way and we are stuck with this world, whatever our views about it. Science is therefore not concerned to create nature, only to reveal *why* it is as it is. We can describe this 'given' character of nature by saying it is an *objective* world. It exists, as a matter of fact, independently of any *subjective* feelings we may have about it. This is why science itself proceeds in an objective fashion. It seeks to discover what *is,* not what *ought* to be. How does it do this?

The method which scientists try to follow in principle is called the *'Hypothetico-Deductive'* method. The stages in this method are as follows. From existing knowledge—what is—the scientist speculates what might *also* be. This is called the deduction of an *hypothesis.* (The term 'hypothetico-deductive' comes from this of course). For example, say we know that, on average, men contract lung cancer more often than women. Say we also know that, on average, men smoke more cigarettes than women. Knowing these facts, we might well speculate *(hypothesise)* that smoking causes lung cancer. It is not that there are not other potential (hypothetical) explanations of these facts. For example, it could be that men tend to work at jobs which make lung cancer more likely. Or it could be that men have some kind of biological disposition towards cancer which women do not possess. There are always plenty of alternative, competing, hypotheses of the causes of things. Scientists have to choose the explanation they think most likely.

But simply choosing an explanation out of personal preference, or intuition, would not get us very far by itself. It is true that there are many occasions when human beings say they 'know' things to be true when what they really mean is that they 'think' it to be true. This would be the case if I were to say that I 'know' the Labour Party will win the next election, for example. Science aims at much greater certainty in its explanations than this, however. Having arrived at an hypothesis—a plausible or appealing story about how something or other is caused—scientists do not then spend their time trying to persuade us of its truth by the logic of their argument, as philosophers do. Nor do they ask us to simply have faith in their belief, as theologians sometimes do. They try to *prove* its truth to us. This they do by *showing* it to be true. How do they do this?

Science only accepts as a true—or, as it is called in science, a *valid*—explanation about reality one which has been demonstrated to be true by the support of *empirical,* or observable, evidence. To put this in scientific language, the scientific method involves the testing of an as yet unverified explanation of reality against the empirical evidence. For example, however much you hate the smell of cigarette smoke, you cannot show the hypothesis that smoking causes lung cancer to be true simply by saying you would like it to be true. Whether we approve of smoking or not is irrelevant. Scientifically we can only say it is true if we can muster the evidence to demonstrate it to be true.

How does this testing of an hypothesis—the examination of the empirical evidence—take place? Scientific investigation involves the testing of the validity of hypotheses by means of the *experiment.* Though a few sciences test hypotheses by looking at phenomena in their natural environment alone most sciences are experimental sciences.

A scientific experiment involves removing the phenomena in which you are interested—called the experimental variables—from their natural setting and examining them, under controlled conditions, in a laboratory. The idea is sensible enough. Since an hypothesis specifies a cause and effect relationship between particular variables, these variables should be examined in isolation from others. If, when variables which are irrelevant to the hypothesis—called extraneous variables—are not present, an hypothesised effect does come about, the hypothesis has been supported.

The aim of an experiment is to measure the degree or extent to which a cause and effect relationship exists. This is how Cuff and Payne put it: "In the ideal experiment, the scientist can control all important variables except one, and then see what happens when that one is varied. For example, if we wish to study the effects of a certain chemical on the growth of runner beans, or if we wish to test a specific hypothesis to the effect that the presence of this chemical and plant growth have a stated relationship, then 'all' other factors, for example, sunlight, water, seed, soil, must be the same for all the sample plots. Then, the varying amounts of the chemical on different test plots can be held responsible for the different growth rates observed of the runner beans. By controlling the conditions, that is 'other factors', we have a method of observing and comparing which allows us to infer specific causal relationships."

Positivist Sociology

The desire to use positivist procedures in sociology has a long history. Auguste Comte, the Frenchman who first of all called the subject sociology, saw science as the answer to societal reconstruction. For him, since science had enabled humans to understand the laws which governed nature and to harness natural processes for their benefit, so sociology—the science of society—would reveal the laws governing social behaviour and allow society to be reconstructed correctly.

In the nineteenth and early twentieth centuries the positivist flag was flown most exuberantly by Comte's successor, and France's most famous sociologist, Emile Durkheim. During the 20th century positivism in sociology took strongest hold in the U.S., alongside the rise to dominance of structural-functionalism. Why should this be? Why should the desire to be scientific in the study of society be so characteristic of the consensus tradition?

The main reason why consensus theorists have been so keen to use positivist methods is because they consider their subject matter—social structures—to be as objective and as given as is nature. For them, social structures are as given for their inhabitants who encounter them at birth as is the natural world for the phenomena—animate and inanimate—who make *it* up. Daffodils do not choose to be yellow, frogs do not choose to croak and have bulging eyes, water does not choose to freeze. They do nevertheless. This is just 'how things are'. Humans do not choose to have two eyes, a nose and a mouth. Nor do they choose to have two arms and two legs. These are simply biological facts of life.

For consensus theorists, the same is true of society. We do not choose to believe the things we believe or to act in the way we act. We *learn* to think and do these things. Pre-existing cultural rules *determine* our ideas and behaviour through socialisation. Thus, in the same way as natural phenomena are the product of laws of nature, so people's ideas and actions are caused by those external social forces which make up social structures. Because of this similarity between the two kinds of subject-matter—nature and society—the consensus theorist argues that the means by which they are investigated should be similar too.

Structural-consensus theory and positivist practice

It is not surprising that this connection between consensus theory and positivist method was first most powerfully articulated by the original classic consensus theorist, Emile Durkheim. In a work called *The Rules of Sociological Method,* Durkheim rejects the suggestion that the social world can be investigated by reference to non-empirical phenomena. For him, social behaviour is not caused by mysterious metaphysical or theological forces, and certainly not by psychological ones. This essentially positivist position he links unambiguously to structural theory.

Durkheim argues that a society is a normative structure of what he calls 'social facts'. In his own words social facts are 'external to and constraining upon' the individual. This is the orthodox consensus position, of course. The social world is a pre-existing cultural entity for its members. It is through socialisation that these 'external' cultural phenomena—Durkheim's social facts—come to determine (exercise 'constraint' over) people's ideas and behaviour.

Why should this conception of society lead to a belief in the value of positivism to investigate it? Durkheim's argument is this. Since social facts exist independently of people's minds, they should be capable of being investigated independently of their minds too. That is, as factual, objective phenomena, they should be as capable of being observed empirically as are the equally objective and external phenomena which make up the natural world. In Durkheim's words: "The laws of societies are no different from those governing the rest of nature and the method by which they are discovered is identical with that of the other sciences." Stating the need for the empirical study of social life is one thing. Showing how empirical evidence of it can be acquired is another. How do we get at observable evidence of these external cultural forces? Sometimes it can be done easily enough. Some social influences are as visible as is nature. For example, Acts of Parliament (laws) are written down in the Statute Book.

But nearly all social facts do not have such an empirical existence. How can *they* be investigated scientifically? For Durkheim and positivist researchers since, the answer is simple enough. Since behaviour and belief are determined by external structural forces, all we have to do is to discover the number of times people do or say they think things. What we then have is empirical evidence of the forces that have produced this behaviour and belief. A social science can proceed just like a natural science. Hypotheses can be tested against empirical evidence. But how is this empirical evidence to be collected in a social science?

Methods of data collection in positivist sociology

The Experiment

There are two obvious problems here. First, it is hardly ever possible to conduct sociological experiments into the social behaviour of humans. It

Theory and Method in Sociology

is true that social psychology does use the experiment, apparently successfully. In controlled conditions, as in the natural scientist's laboratory, a particular aspect of human behaviour is examined in order to gain observed evidence of its cause. A good example is Stanley Milgram's investigation into obedience.

Milgram was particularly interested in how people will follow instructions, even if they make no sense to them, provided they are issued by someone in authority—that is, someone they expect knows what they are doing. He invited members of the public to take part in a memory experiment. A person turning up at the laboratory was introduced to one of Milgram's assistants posing as another member of the public, and with whom he or she was to partner in the experiment. The 'planted' person claimed to have a weak heart.

Both are shown the equipment to be used and the 'plant' (apparently by chance) draws the assignment of memorising a list of word pairs. In the event of a failure of memory he or she is to be 'punished'. The plant is hooked up to wires in an adjacent room, while the *bona fide* member of the public is told what to do—to administer an electric shock whenever a question is answered wrongly. The subject is shown an electric device which can administer from 15 to 450 volt shocks. In addition it is marked from 'slight shock' to 'Danger: Severe Shock'. The subject is given a 'slight shock' in order to draw the contrast with the severe shock. The 'plant' will in fact receive no shocks at all of course, but the person administering the shocks *does not know that*.

The experiment begins. The plant gets the answers wrong and the subject is told to give shocks at ever increasing voltages. The 'plant' screams and shouts but the subject is told to go on. Eventually the 'plant' is silent but the subject is told to continue; the experimenter will be responsible for what might happen. Over 50% of subjects followed the experiment to the end, giving 450 volt shocks.

Clearly, this kind of experimentation is only feasible in the case of extremely small scale and specific interests. Most sociological research is not of this sort however. Sociologists are interested in things like family behaviour or achievement in education or behaviour in the workplace and so on. Even if they would let us, there would be no point in extracting members of families or schoolkids or carworkers from their normal social settings and observing them under experimental conditions to get empirical evidence of their behaviour. Obviously, they will only exhibit the behaviour in which we are interested in their normal surroundings—at home, in school, at work.

Another problem is that it is hardly ever *desirable* to perform sociological experiments anyway. Quite apart from the (fairly understandable) objections our guinea-pigs might make to being observed for experimental purposes, there is no reason to believe that thinking humans will always reproduce their normal behaviour when they know they are being observed. This problem—the possibility of an alteration in peoples' behaviour when they know they are being observed—is known as the 'observer effect'.

Observation

Being unable to experiment has sometimes led positivist sociologists to carry out non-controlled, non-experimental observation instead. The idea is to test hypotheses by observing the life of the people in whose behaviour you are interested and getting empirical evidence that way. Clearly, the success of observation as a positivist method of data collection depends upon the number of people about whom you want evidence. Only in very small scale settings can an observer hope to be able to get sufficient evidence to properly judge hypotheses.

Observation for positivist purposes has been most influentially carried out by anthropologists. Anthropology is typically interested in small-scale community life, particularly among primitive peoples. *Participant observation*—observation by joining in the lives of your subjects—was established as an indispensible anthropological technique by the first fully-fledged anthropological fieldworker, Bronislaw Malinowski. When war broke out in 1914, Malinowski was on his way to Australia. As an Austrian citizen he was in danger of being interned as an enemy alien. He avoided this by persuading the Australian authorities to allow him to spend the duration of the war on the Trobriand Islands. (As we said in Chapter 2, these lie off the south-east tip of New Guinea). Quite by chance therefore, the first long-term use of participant observation in anthropology took place. Since then, Malinowski's fieldwork has become the usual model for anthropological research.

Nearer to home a similar use of observation has been characteristic of what are known as 'community studies'. In both America and the U.K. these have usually been long-term studies of small communities carried out along anthropological lines. The choice of locations for this kind of research shows how difficult it is to use observation on its own to reveal social structures in any but very small-scale and static settings. These are nearly always rural communities, though it has been used in larger settings, alongside other techniques, in both Britain and America. The two studies of Banbury in Oxfordshire *(Tradition and Change* and *Persistence, Power and Change)* and the community studies of Lloyd

Warner in the U.S. are good examples of this.

Elsewhere in structural sociology, participant observation on its own has tended to be used only in settings more or less equivalent to the tiny village—for example the workgroup (as in Tom Lupton's *On the Shop Floor* and Huw Beynon's *Working for Ford)* or the gang (as in William Foote Whyte's *Street Corner Society).*

The problem of what is known as 'observer effect' is a real one in this kind of *non*-experimental observation too, of course. How can you be sure your subjects are not behaving differently because they know you are there? Anthropologists have tended to argue that because they stay so long in their communities, any danger of them altering the behaviour of their subject by their presence inevitably recedes over time and eventually disappears. However, other observers have argued that you can only minimise your impact on behaviour by pretending you are *not* an observer. Such hidden or 'covert' observation has been used in community studies. For example, Vidich and Bensman *(Small Town in Mass Society)* lived in Springdale, Mass. in the U.S.A. without owning up about their sociological interests. The ethics behind such disguised research are qustionable however. Indeed, many observers prefer to run the risk of their participation influencing their data rather than compromise the confidences of their subjects.

One of the main practical problems with observation for positivist purposes, however, is not to do with ethics or the contamination of the evidence. It concerns numbers. Where the numbers of people in whom you are interested are too large for you to observe them all you have to collect evidence to test your hypotheses some other way.

The Survey

Almost always this is done by asking people questions. Instead of observing their lives directly, you carry out a *survey,* asking your subjects to report on them for you—or, at least, those aspects in which you are interested. The idea is then to collect together all the answers of the people you have surveyed, convert these into quantities (statistics) and then experiment with these answers to discover any significant causal relationships. This is called *Multi-variate Analysis.*

For example, say you are carrying out research into voting behaviour. As part of this research, you hypothesise that there is a causal relationship between gender and voting behaviour. In your survey you ask your subjects how they voted in previous elections. Once you have collected together the answers, you can measure support for your hypothesis. You will know that a % of men voted Tory, b % Labour and c % Liberal/SDP; whereas x % of women voted Tory, y % Labour and z % Liberal/SDP. You can then judge whether your figures show that there is a significant relationship between gender and voting.

But even if there is, you then have to decide if it is a *causal* relationship. For example, it may be that you find more women than men vote Tory. But is this *because* they are women? Or is it for some other reason? For example, is it because more women than men do non-industrial jobs, and it is their job experience which is the causal factor? As we said earlier, there are always alternative hypotheses to be judged. The only way to decide which one should be supported is to test them all against the evidence. In our example, if, having tested the hypothesis that there is a relationship between occupation and voting we find that it is stronger than that between gender and voting, we may feel *this* is the explanation we should support.

As in all science then, the job of the researcher is to examine all possible explanations—alternative hypotheses—against the evidence, in order to *demonstrate* their relative strengths. This is why this is called multivariate analysis. It is the analysis of the relationship between a multiplicity of variables. The point is that the choice of an explanation is not made on a whim but in the light of the evidence.

The results of multi-variate analysis in positivist sociology take a form familiar in all scientific research. Tables, graphs, histograms etc., are all routinely used as pictorial images measuring the extent of causal relationships.

Sometimes the evidence with which we wish to experiment in order to test hypotheses is already in statistical form. Such *official statistics* are the statistics collected by various agencies—governmental, business and charitable—for their purposes but which can be used by social scientists to test their hypotheses. The Census, carried out every ten years, is always a good source of basic data about Britain's population as a whole. In addition, there are a whole range of statistics about various categories within the population which can usefully be used for positivist purposes. Criminal statistics, health statistics, educational statistics, divorce statistics etc. etc. can all be experimented with to assess the plausibility of alternative hypothetical explanations.

Most of the time however, there are no official records of the incidence of ideas and behaviour in which sociologists are interested. It is in these cases that surveys are carried out to provide the evidence. But it should not be thought that all surveys are of the same type. Some are deliberately designed to produce easily analysable data, some are not.

The ease with which statistical analysis of the answers to survey questions can take place depends upon the degree of structure of the survey. Some surveys are carried out by printed questions, in a *questionnaire,* usually sent by post. Obviously all the questions in a questionnaire are exactly the same for each *respondent.* That is, they are completely *structured.*

In an *interview,* which is the normal means by which surveys are carried out, the questions are often structured—asked in exactly the same way for each respondent—too. Structured questions are either closed-ended or open-ended. In closed-ended questions, respondents' answers are categorised from a range of alternatives provided, as in this example.

Q If there were a general election tomorrow who would you vote for?

                                    Conservative
                                    Labour
                                    Liberal
                                    S.D.P.
                                    Alliance
                                    Nationalist

Other (State) _____

                                    Don't know
                                    Too young to vote
                                    Would not vote
                                    (Refused information)

In open-ended questions, respondents answer in any way they like. Open-ended replies in interviews are recorded verbatim. For example:

Q When you hear someone described as 'upper class', what sort of person do you think of?

    PROBE: What other sorts of people do you think of as upper class?
    RECORD FULLY.

Closed-ended questions allow *pre-coding.* This means that a code is attached to each possible answer to a question. The interviewer rings the appropriate answer(s) and a respondent's total closed-ended responses can be easily transferred into a computer. This allows easy multi-variate analysis. For example:

Q How is it that people come to belong to the class that they do?
    DO NOT PROMPT.

Born into it/inheritance/family	01
Innate ability	02
Hard work/achievement	03
Work/job/position	04
Education	05
Income/standard of living	06
Possessions (eg home ownership)	07
Other (specify) _____	08

CODE *ALL* THAT APPLY

Questions taken from *The British Questionnaire:* The International Project on Class Structure and Class Consciousness, British Project, Technical Paper 3, University of Essex, Dept. of Sociology. (D. Rose, G. Marshall, H Newby, C. Vogler 1984).

Such structured questions cannot allow respondents to answer in a very meaningful or elaborate way, however. If an understanding of a respondent in greater depth is considered more important than easy statistical analysis then a focused or unstructured interview may be used instead. A focused interview is centred around particular topics but there is no structure to the questions and no restriction on how deeply a topic might be investigated.

An unstructured interview is really no more than a conversation, and is sometimes used by positivists for exploratory purposes. Where the researcher does not have enough information about the subject matter it will not be possible to write a structured schedule or questionnaire designed to test specific hypotheses. A few unstructured interviews with well-placed and informative respondents is often the best way of acquiring enough knowledge to be able to conduct a structured survey.

There is another reason why less than fully structured interviews are used too. Structured interviews do not allow a full exploration of attitudes and ideas. Though open-ended questions can do the job to an extent the most in-depth way of examining ideas rather than behaviour is by using a focussed or an unstructured interview.

Herein lies the basic dilemma for the survey researcher. The more structured the technique, the easier can the results be analysed statistically. The more unstructured the technique, the greater the likelihood of in-depth understanding, particularly of ideas and attitudes.

Theory and Method in Sociology

These choices are usually portrayed something like this:

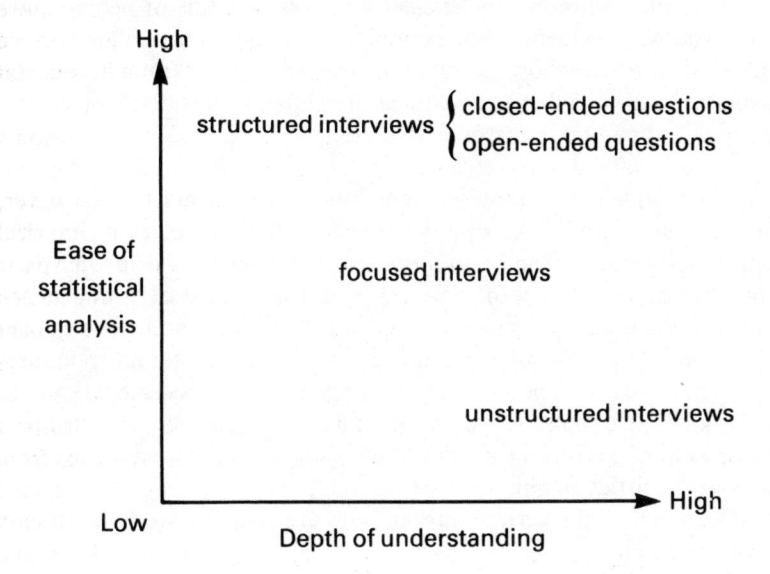

```
High
 |
 |         structured interviews  { closed-ended questions
 |                                 { open-ended questions
 |
Ease of
statistical        focused interviews
analysis
 |
 |                           unstructured interviews
 |
 |                                              High
 |_____→
Low         Depth of understanding
```

Sampling

Another factor also influences the kind of survey conducted. The point of a survey is to compare the results. Often the population about whom you want to make general statements is extremely large. It could be the whole country, all the inhabitants of a town, all the consumers of a particular product, all television watchers or whatever. In such circumstances it is clearly impossible to ask questions of everyone in whom you are interested. What is needed is a *sample* of respondents which is *representative* of the whole. In many circumstances even this sample will need to be fairly sizeable to ensure representativeness. This too will tend to encourage the use of structured interviews. Since they take less time than unstructured ones you can do more of them.

A simple random sample is one in which everyone in your population has an equal chance of inclusion. How the sample is drawn ensures randomness. Picking the required number out of a drum is acceptable. Choosing everyone whose surname begins with the letter J is not.

A stratified random sample is one in whch a random sample is drawn from within different categories of people in the population. This technique is used if you think that a simple random sample will not guarantee the inclusion of sufficient numbers of kinds of people about whom you want evidence. For example, every 50th name on an electoral register in a town whose population over 18 is 10 000 might well not include enough members of political or religious minorities, or old age pensioners, or immigrants or whatever.

A quota sample is the technique most often used by market researchers and newspaper and T.V. opinion pollsters. This involves giving each interviewer a quota from within pre-selected categories of people—e.g. x number of females, y of males, z of old people, a of young people etc.—leaving them to decide how and with whom to meet these quotas.

The problem with all sampling is to ensure representativeness by eliminating *bias*. The people you do interview must accurately represent the bulk of the population you do not interview. An over-representation of one kind of person means that the results will be biased in favour of the characteristics of this kind of person.

To eliminate bias certain precautions are usually taken by sample survey researchers.

1 The list of the whole population from which the sample is drawn *(the sampling frame)* must be accurate.
2 The size of the sample *(the sampling fraction)* must be sufficient.
3 The conduct of the survey must proceed properly. Only selected respondents should be interviewed. If, at the first attempt to locate someone, he or she is unavailable, you do *not* interview the spouse or the man next door who is mowing the lawn instead. At least three attempts at contact should be made. Only then is a substitute interviewed; ideally this should be taken from a sample of the same size held in reserve for this purpose. A certain amount of non-response is inevitable—people die, move house, go on holiday, refuse to be interviewed etc. Non-response in postal questionnaire surveys is always higher than in interview surveys.

   Interviews should all take place over as short a period of time as possible, so that the survey is a snapshot of the population. Dragging it out can mean the passage of time may affect the result; for example it is illegitimate to compare results of questions asked of different people with a three month gap between them.

Assuming all these precautions against bias are taken, the positivist sociologist argues that the sample survey is an indispensable instrument of data collection for a scientific sociology. This is because it allows a carefully-chosen minority to represent the whole and because the results of the survey can be experimented upon with as much rigour as the natural scientist is able to muster in the laboratory.

Anti-Positivist Sociology

Anti-positivist sociologists see things rather differently. Consensus theorists argue that science must be used to explain social life because of the similarity they see between nature and society. It is because *interpretivists* argue the opposite—that social life is nothing like nature—that they insist sociology abandon any attempt to be scientific. For interpretivism, the behaviour of human beings is not determined, as structural theories suggest. It is the product of how people interpret the world around them. It is chosen as appropriate behaviour in the light of how people define the situations they encounter—what they take social settings to *mean*.

According to the interpretivist, because behaviour originates in actors' interpretations of reality, sociological research should be concerned with gaining *understanding* of these interpretations. This can only be done by taking advantage of being human, putting yourself in the place of the actor, and working out how these interpretations were arrived at. In sociology this process is usually called *'verstehen'*.

This is very different from objectively testing hypotheses against empirical evidence. For interpretivists, sociology should be non-scientific—*anti*-positivist. Interpretive sociology's subject-matter—the meanings behind people's actions—is *non*-empirical. The researcher, far from being objective, should be as *sub*jective as possible. Natural scientists do not have to *be* daffodils or rocks or fish or atoms to arrive at cause and effect explanations about such phenomena based on empirical evidence. Indeed, the only way 'true' explanations can be arrived at is to keep as distant from your subject matter as possible. This is what objectivity means.

For interpretivists however, it is only *because* we are part of our subject matter—because we, too, are human—that we have any chance at all of understanding the reasons for our human subjects' actions.

From this point of view, doing sociological research is no different from being a social actor living in the world. All interaction between humans involves 'putting oneself in the place of the other'. That is, to live with, and interact with, one another, we *all* have to employ 'verstehen' all the time. To know how to *re*act to someone's actions, we have to *understand* these actions.

Thus, in contrast to the positivist aim of measurement involving the collection of *quantitative* data, the anti-positivist aim is to understand, and involves the collection of *qualitative* data. We will look at symbolic interactionist methods and ethnomethodological methods separately.

Methods of data collection in anti-positivist sociology
1 Symbolic interactionism

How should this understanding be arrived at? How is verstehen achieved?

Talk

All interpretation involves making sense of things—deciding they 'mean' something or other. As we said in Chapter 1, though we use dress, gesture, touch and even smell to communicate meaning, the most sophisticated way we do so is through language. For this reason interactionist research is typically very interested in what people say. What they say stands for what they mean—what the interactionist is interested in.

Obviously, talking can take place in an interview. But unlike the positivist use of the interview, the point is not to gain evidence of specific ideas and activities we have decided *we* want to investigate. It is to explore the way our subject-matter sees the world. Unlike the positivist, we want no preconceived ideas therefore. We want no leading questions. We do not want our actors to go where *we* lead them. We want to go where they lead us. If interviewing is used in interactionist research then, it is almost always as unstructured as possible.

Writing about their research into the views and perceptions of their lives held by long-term prisoners in Durham jail—the prisoners' 'subjective experience of imprisonment' as they call it—Cohen and Taylor describe the advantages of unstructured over more structured interviewing to reveal actors' meanings as follows. "The techniques that we used were only variants of those which are commonly employed to prompt discussion, e.g. in seminars or at parties and social gatherings. But such everyday usage does not in any way disqualify them as research methods. Indeed we would regard the circumspection of talk which is imposed by more structured methods ... as essentially more intuitive, in that it necessarily involves the *researcher's* assuming that *his* questions are salient to the dimensions he explores and that the answers can be read as 'complete' responses" (my emphasis).

For many interactionists however, even such unstructured talking between sociologist and subjects as this does not avoid the danger they think is always present in question-asking of any kind. This is the equivalent of the 'observer effect' in observation. Their argument is this. Just as the presence of the observer in observation may influence the behaviour of the actors so the presence of the interviewer in interviewing may influence what the subject says. This is an 'interviewer effect'. Cohen and Taylor refer to one aspect of this problem. "... we soon became aware of the subtle and not so subtle ways in which the researcher influences his data by telling the subject enough to produce the definitions of reality he wants to hear about anyway. This is, after all, a feature of most structured talk; when a friend comes to 'talk his problems over' with us, we pick up enough clues to know what response is wanted: sympathy, advice, or a sharing of our own problems."

Other interactionists have pointed out a more general problem with interviewing in sociological research. In recent years both social psychologists and sociologists have produced a lot of evidence demonstrating that respondents tend to give the answers they do to questions about their behaviour and beliefs not because this is the 'truth' but because *these are the answers they want the questioner to hear*. Why should this be? Sometimes it is easily understood. It is a bit much to expect undetected child molesters and mass murderers to happily reveal these aspects of their lives to complete strangers carrying out a research interview. But many interactionists have argued that there is a much more general interviewer effect to be aware of than this. Indeed, they say, we should expect a lack of candour to be normal in *all* interviewing.

Their argument is based on acknowledging the existence of what their theoretical position assumes is an inevitable part of every piece of social interaction. We described it like this in Chapter 4: "... since we soon come to learn that others will interpret our behaviour, our *own* interpretive abilities allow us to manipulate these interpretations to suit our vision of ourselves. We use our capacity to be *self-reflexive* in order to present the person we wish others to think we are. We play roles in a *creative* way to elicit from others the responses we desire. In effect, we manage, or orchestrate, the responses of others by presenting the image of our self we wish them to hold. We become actors on the stage of life, writing our own lines."

If this *is* a part of every piece of social interaction as the interactionist argues, we should hardly expect it to not happen in a piece of interaction which we call an interview. Indeed, since interviews are usually conducted between complete strangers, such 'impression management', as Goffman terms it, is probably more likely than in interaction between acquaintances. That is, we should *expect* the answers to our questions to be those our respondents want us to hear. Furthermore, what they want us to hear will be the result of their interpretation of us—what kind of person they have decided we are.

Though sometimes people want us to think bad things about them and deliberately set out to offend us, it is more usual for people to structure their behaviour to seek our approval. This is supported by the evidence from research into research interviews. This shows that one of the most common sources of distortion in interview research is what is sometimes called the 'desirability effect'. Here a respondent's replies are those he or she thinks the interviewer will approve of. In effect, a desire to be thought well of outweighs any impulse to tell the truth.

For many interactionists, this problem is inherent in all kinds of interviewing as a source of data and is not only a damning indictment of the more structured question-asking techniques used in survey research but makes *any* interview—however informal—likely to be a source of distortion rather than revelation.

For this reason, much interactionist research has abandoned deliberate question-asking as a data collection technique. Instead, such researchers have taken verstehen to its logical conclusion. To understand the meanings which underpin the actions of someone else, you become as much like that person as it is possible to be. To understand the actor's view of the world, you become that actor as far as you can.

Participant observation

This is why interactionists use participant observation. Unlike positivists, e.g. anthropologists, who use the technique to reveal the structural forces determining behaviour and belief, the anti-positivist purpose is to use it to experience reality as the subject experiences it.

The following accounts of the rationale behind the use of participant observation in two well-known interactionist studies—Howard Becker's of life in a medical school, *The Boys in White* and Erving Goffman's famous study of life in a mental hospital contained in *Asylums*—clearly show how the interactionist's desire to understand the actors' view of the world demands the participation of the researcher in their lives. From *Asylums* (Preface): "My immediate object in doing fieldwork at St. Elizabeth's was to try to learn about the social world of the hospital inmate, as this world is subjectively experienced by him. I started out in the role of an assistant to the athletic director, when pressed avowing to be a student of recreation and community life, and I passed the day with patients avoiding sociable contact with the staff and the carrying of a key. I did not sleep in the wards, and the top hospital management knew what my aims were.

It was then and still is my belief that any group of persons—prisoners, primitives, pilots or patients—develop a life of their own that becomes meaningful, reasonable, and normal once you get close to it, and that a good way to learn about any of these worlds is to submit oneself in the company of the members to the daily round of petty contingencies to which they are subject."

From Becker: *Sociological Work*. Chap. 2 Problems of Inference and Proof in Participant Observation: "The participant observer gathers data by participating in the daily life of the group or organisation he studies. He watches the people he is studying to see what situations they ordinarily meet and how they behave in them. He enters into conversation with some or all of the participants in these situations and discovers their interpretations of the events he has observed."

"... in studying a medical school. We went to lectures with students taking their first two years of basic science and frequented the laboratories in which they spend most of their time, watching them and engaging in casual conversation ... We followed these students to their fraternity houses and sat around while they discussed their school experiences. We accompanied students in the clinical years on rounds with attending physicians, watched them examine patients on the wards and in the clinics, sat in on discussion groups and oral exams. We ate with the students and took night call with them. We pursued interns and residents through their crowded schedules of teaching and medical work. We stayed with one small group of students on each service for periods ranging from a week to two months, spending many full days with them ..."

Here then is a thoroughly *anti*-positivist, *non*-scientific emphasis in sociological investigation. It is far removed from a concern with *non*-involvement in order to remain objective and an exclusive reliance on empirical evidence (perfectly proper if you consider your subject-matter to be forces external to the actors in whom you are interested). The interactionist preoccupation is with as much involvement as possible and an exclusive pursuit of the understanding of a *non*-empirical subject matter—actors' meanings.

Furthermore, this is done by simply being human. Only by taking advantage of being a human being yourself can you put yourself in the place of the actor in whom you are interested and arrive at an understanding of how interpretation gives rise to action in social life.

From this discussion so far, it would seem reasonable to expect interactionists to rely exclusively on participant observation with, at the very most, the occasional addition of informal question-asking in unstructured conversation. But doing so leaves interactionists with something of a problem. Being fully immersed in the world of their actors, they only finish the job when satisfied they have properly understood, as Goffman describes it, the "tissue and fabric of social life". But how do they persuade *others* they have done so? How do interpretivists *prove* they have got the subjective experiences of others correct?

This desire for proof—to *demonstrate* the validity of their understanding to others who were not there—has sometimes led even the most theoretically committed interactionists to use methods and data more usually associated with positivist research. In his celebrated observational study of homosexual activity in public conveniences—called *Tea Room Trade*—Laud Humphreys decided to leave nothing to chance in his efforts to persuade us of the truth of his portrayal. After his two-year long lavatorial stint, he attempted to back up his findings by a sample survey of 100 of the tea-room activists he had observed. (He constructed his frame from car registration numbers). Even Howard Becker in *The Boys in White* produces quantified data to add 'scientific' weight to his observational account.

Among interpretivists, only ethnomethodologists are not faced with this problem of proof. This is why.

Methods of data-collection in anti-positivist sociology
2 Ethnomethodology

The ethnomethodological view is that 'doing sociological research' is no more and no less than another example of the accomplishment of social life by some of the members of the social world. That is, members using common-sense knowledge to understand, and therefore interact with, other members, and sociologists using sociological theories to understand actors' meanings, are engaging in exactly the same kind of social accomplishment. But in neither case can the understanding of the parties to a piece of interaction, whether sociologists or non-sociologists, be said to be 'true', or even necessarily what others might have also understood in the same setting. Understanding is only ever the result of *one* human's ability to make sense of *one* particular social occasion. It cannot be disentangled from the occasion itself, nor from the communicative equipment used by the occasion's participants to make sense of it.

Ethnomethodologically, therefore, 'objective' truth is unobtainable. We have to abandon any search for 'explanations' of social occasions which can be 'proved'. Though, like any other member of society, we can and do arrive at explanations of all the social occasions in which we are involved (whether these are part of sociological research or not), these can only ever be *our* explanations, the product of *our* interpretive efforts.

This is why ethnomethodologists, as we saw in Chapter 4, are led to changing the focus and interest of the sociological enterprise. Hamstrung by their membership of the social world, they believe sociologists can never provide proven explanations of the causes of social phenomena. However, they can reveal the procedures and methods by which humans make sense of the settings in which they find themselves. Indeed, since doing sociological research is another example of precisely this activity, the research act itself can be used as data. That is, though sociologists can never arrive at anything other than a subjective explanation of social life, this does not mean they cannot describe *how* they arrived at this view. In short, instead of verstehen being the instrument sociology uses to understand and explain actors' meanings, it becomes the topic—the object of research—whether used by sociologists or non-sociologists.

How does ethnomethodology go about revealing the methods humans employ to understand each other? Its practitioners have disagreed among themselves about how best to do so.

The Experiment

As we saw in Chapter 4, in the typical ethnomethodological experiment, members' common-sense expectations of the behaviour of others are deliberately confounded, in order to demonstrate the kinds of mechanisms humans rely on to make sense of the settings in which they find themselves. In another well-known Garfinkel experiment, for example, he instructed his students to pretend they were lodgers in their own homes. Faced with their close relations behaving as strangers, Garfinkel suggests that the rest of the families reacted oddly because they had been deprived of one of the essentials for a social existence—the expectation that others will join with you in reaffirming that the world is what you take it as being. Even a very temporary reluctance to join in this ever present task of confirming the 'facts' of existence—in this case, spending fifteen minutes refusing to act in ways which would confirm family membership—is bound to produce bafflement and distress for the other participants in this occasion.

Participant Observation

Other ethnomethodologists argue for the benefits of descriptions, or 'ethnographies' as they call them, of the methods humans employ to make sense of social settings based on observation. These are often of the most mundane, or taken-for-granted activites. 'Doing walking' is the name of one such well-known account. The idea is to show that even in demonstrating competence of the kinds of abilities we take most for granted, the human being is working at a social accomplishment of a complex kind.

Conversational Analysis

In so far as language is the principal method which humans employ to construct their social worlds between them, the description of how this method is employed is obviously a central ethnomethodological interest. This is known as 'conversational analysis'. Harvey Sacks' well-known study of suicide is a good example of this route to 'members' methods'. It also demonstrates how ethnomethodological accounts of social activities bear little or no resemblance to accounts of the same activities from any other theoretical perspective.

In his research, Sacks is not really interested in suicide at all. As in other ethnomethodological studies, the particular activities under scrutiny are only useful as arenas in which the real topic—how social life is accomplished—can be revealed.

Sacks carried out his research by examining transcripts of recorded telephone conversations between potential suicides and staff at a suicide prevention centre. The telephone calls are efforts on the part of the callers to communicate their desperation to the staff at the centre. For Sacks they are demonstrations of how:

1 the callers and the staff members came to an understanding of each other;
2 Sacks himself has to engage in just the same kind of sense-making methods in order to understand the meanings of the transcripts.

The relationship between theory and method: an illustration

J. Maxwell Atkinson: Coroners and the Categorisation of Deaths as Suicides
Changes in Perspective as Features of the Research Process

During the course of his research into suicide, Atkinson shifted his theoretical position completely. Of interest here are the implications of these alterations for the way research should be carried out. By using some of Atkinson's own story of his theoretical development (Atkinson, in Bell and Newby) and by identifying the kinds of influences on this development, we can shed some light on the relationship between theory and method in sociology and on the big differences in positivist and anti-positivist research procedures.

Stage 1 — Positivism

At the beginning, Atkinson was concerned to discover the structural causes of suicide. Because of this he engaged in ordinary positivist research. As we have seen, most positivist research involves the analysis of statistics collected by means of social surveys. The study of suicide, however, obviously demands the employment or rather different routes to such empirical evidence. In one of the earliest, and still famous, studies of the subject, Emile Durkheim used the official suicide statistics between the years 1866-78.

Durkheim's 'Suicide'. From an examination of these statistics, three conclusions were immediately apparent to him.
1   within single societies the rate of suicide remains remarkably constant.
2   the rate varies between societies.
3   the rate varies between different groups within the *same* society.
According to Durkheim the only possible hypothesis to be deduced from this is that suicide has structural origins. That is, variations in the suicide rate reflect different structural influences on the members of different societies and on different groups within the same society.

Having been lead to this general conclusion by an examination of the statistics, Durkheim constructs a more detailed hypothesis of the way in which suicide is structurally determined. This hypothesis explains what kinds of group will have higher suicide rates and what kinds of group will not. He argues that the rate of suicide among different groups or societies depends upon their degree of *'social integration'* and *'moral regulation'*.

By 'social integration' he means the degree to which values, attitudes, beliefs and patterns of behaviour are shared among the members of a social group. By 'moral regulation' he means the way in which society controls the desires of individuals through socialisation; that is, the way in which norms and values constrain people's behaviour.

Having defined his concepts, Durkheim then hypothesises that "suicide varies ... with the degree of integration of the social group of which the individual forms a part" and sets out to examine its empirical validity. He does this by means of a detailed scientific examination of the suicide statistics, according to the canons of scientific enquiry.

As a laboratory scientist would, Durkheim measures the relationship between what he hypothesises are his causal or *independent* variables—the degree of integration and moral regulation of a social group—and the variable he believes is affected by this factor—the *dependent* variable—the rate of suicide in the group.

He examines this hypothetical relationship in a range of groups included in the statistics. Eg. he looks at family, religious, political and occupational groups, at groups at different times in a society's history, at different societies, and at different societies at different times in their history. Cuff and Payne describe part of this multivariate analysis as follows: "Durkheim starts by studying the publicly available information, the official statistics, on the rate of suicide for various countries in Europe. He notes that suicide is much more common in Protestant countries than in Catholic countries. In trying to establish the extent religious persuasion is linked with suicidal tendencies, Durkheim's problem resembles that of the researcher in the laboratory: how to control the conditions. In the above example, it could be that being Protestant is causally linked to a tendency to commit suicide, but it could also be that being German is the real determining agent. What Durkheim does is to hold nationality constant. He controls for the influence of the variable 'nationality' by comparing the influence of the two religions within a single society. For example, he finds that Bavaria has the fewest suicides of all the states of Germany, and it also has the most Catholics. He goes on to strengthen the empirical support for the link by showing that if we compare the provinces within Bavaria, we find that suicides are in direct proportion to the number of Protestants and in inverse proportion to the number of Catholics. In other words, where there are more Catholics there is less suicide, and where there are more Protestants there is more suicide.

Durkheim has by no means proved that being Protestant and the tendency to commit suicide are definitely causally linked. The more times he demonstrates, however, that these two variables 'go together' in different situations, and the more he eliminates third variables (for example, 'nationality' (German), 'region' (Bavaria)), the more empirical support he provides for inferring a causal link.''

Having completed his analysis, Durkheim was satisfied that his hypothesis had been proved correct. He concluded that suicide could be classified into three types, caused by

either: 1 under-integration into the group
or: 2 over-integration into it
or: 3 too little moral regulation.

He called 1 suicide from under-integration *egoistic* suicide
2 suicide from over-integration *altruistic* suicide
3 suicide from too little moral regulation *anomic* suicide

Egoistic suicide

The product of too little integration into a group, according to Durkheim, this explains why, for example, single, widowed or divorced people are more prone to suicide than married people, or why married people without children are more prone than married people with a family.

Again, according to Durkheim, this explains why Protestants are more prone to suicide than Catholics. He argues that Protestants are more often left to make personal and moral choices in their lives than Catholics who belong to a faith which instructs and guides their actions to a far greater degree.

Altruistic suicide

Here, according to Durkheim, people are more prone to suicide the *more* integrated into the group they are. One example is of the Hindu widow who throws herself onto the funeral pyre of her husband so that she will not be a burden on her family now that she is alone. (This is known as 'suttee'.) Another is of soldiers who sacrifice themselves for their fellow soldiers or their country.

Anomic suicide

According to Durkheim, this kind of suicide is likely to happen among people whose socialisation is suddenly no longer appropriate to the new circumstances in which they find themselves. Having learnt one particular type of normative or moral regulation they no longer know how to behave when dramatic alterations in their lives render these rules irrelevant. This, says, Durkheim, makes them prone to despair and suicide. Eg. he argues, this can happen at times of great economic disruption, such as during severe slumps or rapid booms.

In all these cases, so far as he is concerned, Durkheim has demonstrated the externality of the causes of suicide. The impulse to take their own lives lies not inside individuals as some kind of purely psychological or biological phenomenon. Instead it is influenced by the kind of group or society in which individuals find themselves and whose cultural or normative characteristics into which they are socialised promote or encourage the activity.

Because this is the theoretical case, argues Durkheim, it is only scientific methodological procedures—the testing of hypotheses against empirical evidence—which can provide the evidence. In his own words: "the basic proposition that social facts are objective ... finds a new and especially conclusive proof in statistics and above all in the statistics of suicide."

Durkheim's work has been criticised from within positivism. For example, it has been argued that he failed to recognise the over-riding importance of geographical location. This criticism suggests that some of the types of people Durkheim considered most vulnerable—eg. those living alone or of the Protestant faith—are also more likely to live in urban rather than rural areas and it is this that is the decisive causal factor.

This kind of criticism does not argue with the principle of the statistical analysis of suicide, but with the manner in which Durkheim carried it out. As he began his research, Atkinson too (positivistically) accepted that though there were weaknesses in the detail of Durkheim's work, the general approach was right and that it could be improved upon. As he puts it, "By focusing on the way in which suicide statistics were compiled ... the hope was that better rates could be computed so that a more thorough test of Durkheim's theory could be carried out ..." (Bell and Newby).

Stage 2—Interactionism

As his work progressed, however, Atkinson began to shift his theoretical and methodological ground, away from structuralist/positivist assumptions and towards interactionism/anti-positivism. The interactionist critique of positivist approaches to suicide is usually associated with the work of J.D. Douglas.

Douglas: The Social Meanings of Suicide

In this book, Douglas argues that the 'objective' indicators which Durkheim uses as evidence of the external determinants of suicidal behaviour—the official statistics of the rate of suicides among different groups and societies—are in fact no such thing. For him, far from being *objective* social facts these statistics are in reality (like all social phenomena) very much the product of the *subjective* interpretations of particular individuals. His argument runs along these lines.

The way a death becomes a suicide is a complex interpretive process involving particular definitions of situations by particular individuals. (We only have to recall our earlier example in Chapter 1 of how differently two policemen might interpret the death of a car driver to appreciate this.) Since this is so, Durkheim is quite wrong to see these statistics as somehow 'true' indicators of suicide rates which can be analysed scientifically as though they were unproblematic, objective 'facts'. All they can be taken as being are reflections of the *particular* subjective interpretations of unforeseen or unusual deaths arrived at by *particular* people, especially those whose job it is to arrive at such definitions, such as police officers and coroners.

Research into suicide should therefore take a very different form from the positivist emphasis on empirical evidence insisted upon by Durkheim and, initially, by Atkinson. For interactionists, suicides only ever become suicides because of the labels attached to deaths by particular individuals. Therefore we are never going to know the 'facts' of these matters—whether the deaths actually *were* suicides or not.

What we can find out about, however, are the kinds of reasons why certain deaths come to be *labelled* as suicides. We can discover how the definition of a death as self-inflicted is arrived at. And, ironically enough, it is Durkheim's 'objective' indicators of the 'true' rate of suicide—the official statistics—that can help us.

Deaths only become suicides, and therefore, included in the statistics, as a result of a process of official labelling. Since this is so, social research into the subject should concern itself with how and why such labels become attached—how the statistics become compiled. This, of course, is not the construction of empirical evidence of *external social determinants* of behaviour. It is the analysis of a very *non*-empirical activity—the interpretive procedures routinely employed by people in order to make sense of unexpected death.

For the interactionist then, though the evidence remains the same as that used by the positivist—the suicide rates—the topic changes, from an interest in the labelled to an interest in the labellers. As Atkinson says about his conversion to interactionism: "... the question of how some deaths get defined as suicide could remain as a central focus without being inconsistent with the ideas of the new perspective. Whereas originally it had been intended that the investigation would lead to more rigorous ways of doing Durkheimian positivism, it now came to be directed to questions about the different available definitions of suicidal situations and about the social meanings of suicide."

As a consequence of this change of subject-matter, Atkinson's methods changed too, though rather slowly and painfully, and somewhat unintentionally. "The general change in orientation did not, however, provide any immediate solution to the problem of what kind of empirical research should now be done, which is probably one reason why parts of the positivist legacy survived for so long. Another might have had to do with the very obvious difficulties involved in using participant observation to study suicidal phenomena. But I also retained doubts about the vagueness and apparent sloppiness which seemed to characterise some of the research strategies adopted by interactionists: a funny story here, an apt quote from a 'subject' there, a few extracts from a newspaper or television ... This was very different from the ordered way in which survey research could be carried out, and it was not easy to make the decision to forget so many hard-learned principles and exchange them for so vaguely specified an alternative. I therefore began to try ways of organising the research which would be both 'systematic' and relevant to my new found interests. In examining press reports of suicide, for example, the newspaper would be held constant by looking at different issues of the same one over a fixed period of time. Coding was used to collect data from coroners' records, IBM cards were punched, and reasonably large samples were still considered a necessity.

While these various positivistic methods were being deployed in the pursuit of answers to interactionist questions, other 'qualitative' data were steadily and unknowingly being collected. I had obtained access to a coroner's records as a result of an offer from the Essex County Coroner ... Taking advantage of such an offer obviously involved meetings, but on the several occasions when I had lengthy discussions with him neither of us was aware that a 'research interview' was taking place ..."

Stage 3 — Ethnomethodology

Utimately, however, interactionism lost out to ethnomethodology. Atkinson began to believe that the 'truth' about suicide was unobtainable for a member of the social world. Instead, as in ethnomethodological research into anything, the topic became the mechanisms and methods humans (sociologists and non-sociologists) use to make sense of each other and thereby construct social life.

This is how Atkinson describes his final conversion: "... the transition to ethnomethodology was rather more painful than the earlier change of perspective. For not only did it involve discarding some of the most deeply entrenched traditional rationales for doing sociology (eg. to construct decontextualised descriptions and theories of social action which are different from and better than the situated practical descriptions and theories of members), but in addition the new analytic interest was to be in the topic of descriptive procedures rather than in suicide *per se*. Data on suicidal phenomena thus became no more and no less appropriate than data on any other topic describable by members ..."

What about the other kind of theorists who do not subscribe to the structural-consensus view of society? As we said at the beginning of the chapter, it is true that many conflict theorists believe in the value of scientific analysis. Like consensus theorists, conflict theorists see behaviour as the product of external structural factors. In their case, the objective facts of people's lives which determine their behaviour are the *advantages* they possess—their position in the structures of inequality.

These advantages are both material and political: whether one is economically advantaged in material resources or politically so in terms of exercising power, one's position in society can be said to be structurally advantaged. For conflict theorists it is the structure of social relationships in social systems that must be the focus of attention. Though this structure is not something directly 'observable' in a form which positivists would require, the structural relations can be said to be objective, nevertheless, since they can be established independently of people's own conception of social reality. However as *relationships* they are *abstractions* (like Marx's concept of contradiction) and so need a rather different 'scientific method' for revealing them than we have seen in positivism. This could, for example, be a sort of 'functional' analysis as used by much Marxist thought: that is, examining how a system (such as the capitalist system) 'functions' and so determining the sort of relationships (and conflicts) engendered by it. This is not the place to pursue these, often rather complex, methodological problems however.

While not all conflict theorists believe that the strains and inequalities they perceive are eradicable, some (like the Marxian camp) clearly do. This is because of the criticisms of the social order inherent in their analysis. To argue that social structures consist of groups in possession of unequal advantages usually means that the theorist has an image of a better world where inequalities are not so great. Whether it be an explanation of inequalities between men and women, black and white, young and old, rich and poor or whatever, an emphasis on these kinds of structural determinants of behaviour in a sociological theory usually goes hand in hand with a view that such inequalities ought to be reduced or eradicated. The subject-matter, that is the structures of inequality, is *not* given or incapable of being altered. It *can* be changed, and *in a way nature cannot*. For this reason, while conflict theorists are usually quite happy to use structural analysis to provide demonstrable evidence of unequal structures, unlike positivists, they usually have a very definite view of what *ought* to be built into their analysis as well.

Values, Objectivity and Knowledge

It is true that the original positivists, like Comte and Durkheim, also felt that the point of studying society scientifically was to be able to change it for the better. But they did not feel the creation of a better society was a matter of personal judgement. For them there was only one correct society, whose creation depended upon people discovering the laws governing social life. For this reason, science alone can lead to the good society; it is only once we know what 'is' the truth that we will be able to act correctly. This view allocated a crucial role to sociologists. Because it is the scientists of society who discover what *is,* they are the people best placed to prescribe what *ought* to be. Indeed, Comte even went so far as to describe this science as the 'Queen' of the sciences, and its practitioners—sociologists—the 'priests' of a new golden age of proven truth.

By the twentieth century and the establishment of positivism in U.S. sociology, this view of social science and of the social scientist had changed, however. It was still argued that only science can tell us the truth. But truth began to be connected to *value-freedom*. For the twentieth century positivist, only if scientists are completely objective, and deal *only* with the facts, can they discover what is. Furthermore, this value-freedom means not only excluding judgements from the process of discovering the truth. It also means that the social scientists must *not* enter the business of prescribing what ought to be. Scientists, that is, must be neutral. *They* must not take sides.

In contrast to the early positivist sociologists then, who saw themselves as the knowledgeable architects of the perfect society, twentieth century positivism relegated the scientist, whether natural or social, to the role of information-gatherer.

This model of objectivity has come under considerable attack in social science. Objections to it are of two main kinds. The first argues this. To equate objectivity with value-freedom is wrong. Values are bound to enter into the selection of a subject-matter to investigate. They are also bound to enter into the choice of questions to ask about this subject-matter. Nevertheless, this does not mean that objectivity is impossible. The second objection is that the positivist view of the scientist's role as neutral information-gatherer is at best naive and at worst immoral. To imagine that the pursuit of knowledge is best served by scientists suspending their humanity and keeping out of debates about the way things ought to be is both foolish and dangerous. We will look at these two criticisms in turn.

Can a social science be value-free?

A whole range of critics have argued that both the selection of a subject matter to study and the choice of a theoretical perspective to direct its investigation inevitably depend upon value-judgements. A scientist has to make two kinds of selection based on values. To choose an area to investigate reflects a belief that this is worth studying. It means we are deciding it it *better* to know about things such as the causes of cancer or of racial discrimination rather than gender discrimination or the geology of the moon.

More than this, *how* this selected subject-matter is studied inevitably reflects values too. Scientists do not just trawl in facts in some kind of neutral way. Just as fishermen choose one fishing-ground rather than another, so scientists choose to ask certain questions, certain hypotheses, rather than others. The facts collected in scientific research depend upon the questions asked. These questions reflect a theoretical interest. The decision to choose to support one theory as opposed to another is based upon a value-judgement. Nevertheless, objectivity is still possible, so long as two rules are followed. First, we must reveal the values that direct our research, so that others can judge our choices from the point of view of *their* values. Second, so long as values are kept out of the *testing* of a selected hypothesis—a selection based on values—the results can be said to be valid, or true, results. It just is not the whole truth. Other hypotheses could have been tested, other questions could have been asked, instead.

This view of knowledge and its production, most elegantly expressed by Max Weber, raises some interesting questions. Since theoretical preference determines what we collect evidence about and since our values determine this preference, what determines our values will determine our knowledge. We can make three related points here.

From this point of view, knowledge is clearly a cultural product. What is important or, to use Weber's phrase, "worthy of being known", about, in one culture may not be in another culture. If so, one culture will produce one body of knowledge, reflecting its characteristic values. Another culture may consider very different things worthy of being known about.

How values come to prevail in a culture is therefore crucial for the knowledge produced by that culture. It means that the debate between consensus and conflict theorists about the origin and role of values is also a debate about the origin and status of knowledge. Consensus theorists believe that values come to prevail because they are structurally necessary. This implies that a society will produce the *knowledge* it needs. In contrast, conflict theorists believe that values reflect and serve the interests of the powerful. This implies that the knowledge a culture produces will also reflect its power structure. Furthermore, it seems to imply that in an unequal world, knowledge can be ideological. Like other dominant ideas, it can work to benefit the advantaged and disadvantage the weak.

Does this mean that we have no objective way of judging the relative value of different sorts of knowledge? If values are not right or wrong but just different, this seems to suggest that knowledge itself is not more or less important or useful, but just different. This seems to leave us with the rather disturbing conclusion that all truth is relative and we are in no position to judge one kind as objectively superior to another. But many sociologists would totally reject the idea that Hitler's view of humanity and how people should be treated is no better or worse than Mother Theresa's. Does supporting *this* position mean that we have to argue that there *are* 'correct' values?

Should a social science try to be value-free? The role of the sociologist in society

Other critics of the positivist position on value-freedom attack it on slightly different grounds. This argument, closely associated with much conflict theory, strongly criticises the positivist view that in order to produce objective knowledge, social scientists should play no part in making decisions about how the world ought to be.

Many conflict theorists have pointed to the way this value-neutral role has allowed sociologists (and other scientists), in the U.S. in particular, to be used by governmental and business agencies in the pursuit of goals *they* desire. Very common in the 1940's, 1950's and early 1960's, the most infamous case of social science being used in this way was Project Camelot. Begun in 1964, this was a massive research programme, funded by the U.S. Army, designed to reveal the origins of social instability in Latin America. This is how Bilton et al describe the project. "In its natural concern for social order in the lower half of the continent, the Pentagon wished to discover the causes of revolt and remove them. In order to achieve this, they planned to spend up to six million dollars and recruit a huge team of political scientists and sociologists to work in the countries concerned. Their employer made the aims clear in a recruiting letter: 'The U.S. Army has an important mission in the positive and constructive aspects of nation-building in less-developed countries as well as to a responsibility to assist friendly governments in dealing with active insurgency problems'."

The criticism of this kind of social research, carried out for employers who can put it to whatever purpose they desire, is that it is not 'value-neutral' at all. As critics point out, it is not that there are no values involved. It is that the values are employer values, not the values of the sociologist.

A great deal of U.S. sociology this century has been quite happy to allow itself to be bought and used in this way. As one of the most vociferous supporters of a 'value-free' science of society, George A Lundberg put it: "The services of *real* social scientists would be as indispensible to Fascists as to Communists and Democrats ..."

Why should this be? According to Alvin Gouldner, this is not the outcome of a naive, erroneous view of the possibility of producing value-free knowledge. For him, it was the result of a self-interested, cynically amoral view of the practice of doing sociology deliberately chosen by U.S. positivist sociologists. His argument, presented in an article called *Anti-Minotaur—the myth of a value-free sociology,* runs along these lines.

After the first world war, sociology became established as a fully-fledged discipline in the U.S. In the beginning, American sociologists had a reputation as being social reformers, ever-critical of the faults they saw in American society. Those in power in the U.S. resented a social structure from which they benefitted being constantly attacked as in need of reform. They rejected these sociological criticisms as illegitimate, and sociologists as uninformed prejudiced radicals.

As time went on, U.S. sociologists began to be concerned about their degraded status in their society. They craved greater professional and intellectual credibility. They began to think that if the 'critic and reformer' label could be discarded, they would be more acceptable to the establishment and acquire greater importance. But such blatant self-interestedness could not be openly pursued. It had to be dressed up as something else. In this way says Gouldner, the myth of the desirability of a value-free sociology was born. By retreating from debates about what should be done about social issues in America, American sociologists ceased to be seen by the establishment as a threat to their power. Instead of being commentators on social ills, positivist sociologists became merely collectors of facts, with no axes to grind. Free from values and uninterested in changing society, the social scientists left the debates to politicians. As a result, they began to be seen as safe not threatening. They began to secure the respect of the powerful they had craved.

But, says Gouldner, these positivists' 'freedom from values' is in fact a myth. Disengaging from debates about what ought to be does not free sociologists from passing judgement about society. There is no such thing as neutrality in *effect*. Saying nothing encourages nothing to happen, which simply allows things to go on as they are. Saying and doing nothing is in fact supporting the status quo.

Was positivist sociology's value-freedom a mistake then? Gouldner will have none of this. He claims the positivists knew exactly what the consequences of their chosen neutral role would be. They *knew* they would be seen as tacitly supporting the establishment. This was their intention. By insisting on the possibility and the desirability of value-freedom in a social science they were in fact passing on the message to their rulers: "we will not rock your boat". In return for this acquiescence, they were accorded the enhanced social position for their profession which had been their aim all along.

Following Gouldner's lead, much U.S. sociology in the 1960's and early 1970's rejected the inherent conservatism of positivism/functionalism. Instead it argued for a more radical and committed approach to social life. This has taken one of two forms. Symbolic interactionists like Howard Becker have argued for a compassionate sociology, one of the 'underdog'. This is derived from two basic tenets: i we can only know about social behaviour by seeing reality from the point of view of the actor; ii the most disadvantaged in society—the labelled deviant—is only an ordinary person unable to resist the impact of unfavourable circumstances. Since the world as seen by the powerful (the 'overdogs') is well known, sociology should actively balance things up, by taking the underdogs' side and understanding how the world looks to them. That is, we must choose our actors to understand from among the most disadvantaged in society, namely the deviants, who cannot speak for themselves. As Goffman puts it in his preface to *Asylums:* "To describe the patients' situation faithfully is necessarily to present a partisan view. (For this last bias I partly excuse myself by arguing that the imbalance is at least on the right side of the scale, since almost all professional literature on mental patients is written from the point of view of the psychiatrist, and he, socially speaking, is on the other side)".

In contrast to this kind of partisan side-taking sociology of the interactionists, some conflict theorists have argued for a far more self-consciously *politically* radical approach to social life. As we said earlier, often built into a conflict analysis of the structure of inequality in society is a prescription for the removal of these inequalities. This kind of sociology has often been contemptuous of what it considers the rather romantic and sentimental approach to disadvantage of the interactionists. Gouldner himself has attacked Becker for taking too 'safe' an interest in inequalities of power. He accused him of being only concerned with people 'on their backs', like the deviant underdog, rather than with people 'fighting back', like the politically radical.

Here is an injunction for sociology to be 'explicitly political'. Alongside an analysis of the structural sources of disadvantage should be a self-conscious commitment to its eradication. Following Marx's view that science and action can never be separated, the conflict reaction to positivisms's neutrality has generally been to argue that scientific analysis must be pressed into service to change society. Sociologists must be true to their own values. The essence of this position is that choosing a conflict perspective represents a view of the world as not only unequal. It is also *wrongly* unequal. So it is not good enough to simply describe and explain wrongs. Values must be followed through and wrongs must be righted.

Conclusion

This book is unashamedly a book for the beginner. In writing it I have had two priorities. I have tried to provide both a clear framework for understanding the development and characteristics of sociological theory and method and an account that is above all thematic, even if this means doing less than justice to the full complexities of the theoretical and methodological reality. These priorities are reflected in the content and organisation of the book.

I have suggested that theory and method in sociology can usefully be approached by considering two principal issues:
i the adequacy of structural approaches to theory
ii the adequacy of the positivist approach to knowledge.

The adequacy of structural approaches to theory

Here the emphasis has been on the way in which the rise to prominence of conflict and interpretive theoretical alternatives in present-day sociology can usefully be seen as outcomes, at a particular time in the development of the subject, of specific weaknesses in traditional sociology's dominant theoretical approach—structural-functionalism. The argument was this: so long as the origins and characteristics of the essential assumptions of structural-functionalism are understood—that
1 social structures are normative structures;
2 whose origins are explicable in functional/organicist terms—then so can the rise to prominence of its two principal kinds of theoretical competitors.

First, the attraction of an *alternative* structural tradition—structural-conflict theory, represented by Marxist theory—can be understood since Marxist theory:
a opposes a *normative* model of social structure in favour of one emphasising *unequally advantaged* and *conflicting* groups and
b opposes the *functionalist* conception of the origin of normative arrangements explaining them in *ideological* terms instead.

Second, the attraction of an *anti*-structural approach—interpretivism, represented by symbolic-interactionism/labelling theory and phenomenology/ethnomethodology—can be understood since interpretive theories, instead of seeing society as a pre-existing structural entity, see social life as an accomplishment of the capacities of human beings to engage in social interaction by the communication of meaning.

The adequacy of the positivist approach to knowledge

Here the emphasis has been on the way in which
1 structural-consensus sociology emerged and developed as a discipline committed to the application of positivism to the study of society.
2 methodological alternatives in present-day sociology can be usefully seen as inextricably tied to the interpretive and conflict critiques of the consequences for method of the use of consensus theory.

To summarise, then, the overall aims of the book have been deliberately simple. First, I have tried to establish a thematic link between the development of theoretical alternatives in sociology and second to emphasise that this development has had crucial consequences for method—the production of sociological knowledge. I hope you have found this approach useful and that it has encouraged you to embark enthusiastically on a more detailed and sophisticated study of theory and method in sociology.

Examination Questions

All perspectives

1 Explain and illustrate what is meant by the idea of there being different sociological perspectives and how far do these perspectives reflect different assumptions and interests? JMB 1984

2 Modern sociology centres on the contrast between a sociology of the social system and a sociology of social action. Outline and examine the features of these two sociologies. AEB 1983

3 Although there are many different ways of describing social order, it remains the primary concern of all sociology. Briefly describe two contrasting ways in which sociologists have accounted for social order, and demonstrate how far it is fair to say that such concerns must be central to all sociologies. JMB 1980

Functionalism and its critics

1 Using wide-ranging examples, explain and illustrate the main features of functional analysis. What are the strengths and weaknesses of this form of analysis? JMB 1984

2 "Far from what is usually suggested, it could be claimed that sociology exerts a conservative influence on those who study it since it emphasises the inevitability of forms of social organisation under particular conditions and allocates the individual to a passive role in society." Using examples from your own studies, assess this point of view. JMB 1980

Sociology as a science

1 Examine the argument that the logic and methods of the natural sciences are applicable to the study of human society. AEB 1982

2   Examine the view that sociology should be value-free. AEB 1983

3   Can sociologists justifiably claim to be objective?

Methods of research

1   What part does theory play in sociological research? Cambridge 1983

2   Using any one example of your choice, outline and explain the major steps involved in undertaking sociological research and data analysis. To what extent do you think that generalisations should be the primary goal of all sociological research? JMB 1984

3   "Choice of method in sociological research reflects, among other things, theoretical assumptions and practical restraints." In the light of this statement, compare postal questionnaires and face-to-face interviews as methods of sociological research." AEB 1982

4   What are the relative merits and limitations of participant observation and structured interviews as methods of sociological research? Cambridge 1984

Bibliography

Amis, Martin (1974) *The Rachel Papers.*
Anderson, R.J. (1979) *Listening to Conversation* in Meighan R., Skelton I., and Marks T., *Perspectives on Society,* Thomas Nelson.
Aries, Philippe (1973) *Centuries of Childhood,* Penguin.
Atkinson, J. Maxwell (1977) *Coroners and the Categorisation of Deaths as Suicides* in Bell, Colin and Newby, Howard, *Doing Sociological Research.* Allen and Unwin.
Atkinson, J. Maxwell (1978) *Discovering Suicide,* Macmillan.
Barnett, H.G. (1938) *The Nature of the Potlatch, American Anthropologist* Vo. 40.
Becker, Howard et al (1963) *Boys in White,* University of Chicago Press.
Becker, Howard (1970) *Sociological Work,* Transaction Books.
Benedict, Ruth (1935) *Patterns of Culture,* Routledge and Kegan Paul.
Beynon, Huw (1973) *Working for Ford,* Penguin.
Bilton, Tony et al (1981) *Introductory Sociology,* Macmillan.
British Crime Survey, The (1983) H.M.S.O.
Codere, Helen (1950) *Fighting with Property* University of Washington Press.
Cohen, Stan and Taylor, Laurie (1977) *Talking about Prison Blues* in Bell, Colin and Newby, Howard, *Doing Sociological Research,* Allen and Unwin.
Cuff, E.C. and Payne, G.C.E. (1984) *Perspectives in Sociology,* Allen and Unwin.
Douglas, J.D. (1967) *The Social Meanings of Suicide,* Princeton University Press.
Durkheim, Emile (1964) *The Rules of Sociological Method,* Free Press.
Durkheim, Emile (1970) *Suicide* (ed. G. Simpson) Routledge and Kegan Paul.
Durkheim, Emile (1976) *The Elementary Forms of Religious Life,* Allen and Unwin.
Filmer, Paul (1972) on Harold Garfinkel's Ethnomethodology in Filmer, Paul et al *New Directions in Sociological Theory,* Collier-Macmillan.
Goffman, Erving (1968) *Asylums,* Penguin.
Goffman, Erving (1969) *The Presentation of Self in Everyday Life,* Penguin.
Gouldner, Alvin (1975) *Anti-minatour* in Gouldner, Alvin,

For Sociology, Penguin.
Harris, Marvin (1977) *Cows, Pigs, Wars and Witches,* Fontana.
Humphreys, Laud (1970) *Tea Room Trade,* Duckworth.
Lemert, Edwin (1967) *Human Deviance, Social Problems and Social Control,* Prentice-Hall.
Lupton, Tom (1963) *On the Shop Floor,* Pergamon Press.
Malinowski, Bronislaw (1922) *Argonauts of the Western Pacidic,* Routledge and Kegan Paul.
Milgram, Stanley (1974) *Obedience to Authority,* Tavistock.
Newby, Howard et al (1984) *The British Questionnaire: the International Project on Class Structure and Class Consciousness,* British Project, Technical Paper 3, University of Essex, Department of Sociology.
Parkin, Frank (1971) *Class Inequality and Political Order,* Paladin.
Rex, John (1961) *Key Problems in Sociological Theory,* Routledge and Kegan Paul.
Sacks, Harvey (1967) *The search for help: no one to turn to,* in Schneidman, E.S. (ed.) *Essays in Self-Destruction,* Science House.
Schutz, Alfred (1967) Collected Papers, Vol. 1: *The Problem of Social Reality,* Martinus Nijhoff.
Sharrock, Wes (1977) *The Problem of Order,* in Worsley, Peter, *Introducing Sociology,* Penguin.
Stacey, Margaret (1960) *Tradition and Change,* Oxford University Press
Uberoi, J. Singh (1962) *The Politics of the Kula Ring.*
Vidich, and Bensman (1958) *Small Town in Mass Society:* Princeton University Press
Wallis, Roy (1983) in Mann, Michael *The Macmillan Student Encyclopaedia of Sociology*
Weber, Max (1964) *Theory of Social and Economic Organisation* (ed. T. Parsons), Free Press.
Whyte, William Foote (1943) *Street Corner Society,* University of Chicago Press.

INDEX

alienation 58
anti-positivist sociology 93-100, 105-7

bourgeoisie 46-7, 57

C.K.P. index 71
class 43-59
class conciousness 54-57
'clear-up' rate 72
commonsense knowledge 76-77
community studies 86-87
conflict theory 10-15, 20, 22, 39, 41-2, 107-8, 110-113, 114
consensus theory 5-9, 15, 20-1, 22-24, 83-84, 110, 114
conversational analysis 100
culture 5-9, 11-15, 23-25, 48-49, 52-53, 110

deviance amplification 73

epoch 44
ethnomethodology 21, 40, 75-79, 98-100, 106-7
experiment 77-78, 82, 84-86, 99-100

false conciousness 20-21, 22-42
functionalism 20-21, 22-42, 114

historical materialism 43
hoarding behaviour 65
hypothesis 81-82, 86, 88, 90
hypothetico-deductive method 81-82

ideological legitimation 47-55
individualistic explanations 3-4
infrastructure 43, 48
institutionalisation 67-68
interpretive theory 16-21, 40, 60-79, 94-100, 104-107
interview 89-92, 94-96

Index

kula 28-33
Kwakiutl 34-37

labelling theory 21, 40, 63-73, 105-6
labour market 46
labour power 46
latent function 28
lords 45

manifest function 28
marxist theory 15, 20-21, 41, 42-59
masters 45
modes of production 43-47, 54-58
mortification of the self 68
multi-variate analysis 87-89, 101-104

naturalistic explanations 1-3
non-sociological explanations 1-4
norms 7-8

objectivity 81, 83-84, 108-113
observation 86-87, 96-98
observer effect 86-87
official statistics 71-74, 88, 101-105
organismic analogy 24-25
overdogs 69, 112-113

paranoia 66-67
participant observation 96-98
positivism 21, 80-82
positivist sociology 21, 82-93, 101-103
potlatch 33-36
precoding 89-90
Project Camelot 111
proletariat 46-47, 56-58

qualitative data 94
quantitative data 94
questionnaire 89, 90

respondent 89-92
roles 7

sampling 91-93
sampling fraction 92
sampling frame 92
self, presentation of the 62-63
self-image, construction of 61-63
self-report studies 71-72
serfs 45
slaves 45
socialisation 5-9, 11-15, 23-24, 38-39, 48-49, 54, 61-62
social action 17-18, 40
social integration 25, 27, 32-33
social solidarity 25, 27
social structure 5-15, 20-21, 24-25, 48-49, 58-59
social system 24-25, 41, 58-59
stigma 73
suicide 3-4, 101-107
superstructure 43, 48-54
surplus value 47
surveys 87-93
symbolic interactionism 60-75

tithe 45-47
totemism 25-27
Trobriand Islanders 28-33, 86

underdogs 69, 112-113

values 7-9, 48, 58-59
value-freedom 108-113
verstehen 93-99
victim surveys 71